The New Revelation

D0861878

The New Revelation

Sir Arthur Conan Doyle

WITH INTRODUCTION AND AFTERWORD BY
George J. Lankevich, PhD

SQUAREONE
CLASSICS

Cover Designer: Phaedra Mastrocola
Typesetter: Gary A. Rosenberg
Series Consultant: Skip Whitson
In-House Editor: Marie Caratozzolo

Square One Publishers
Garden City Park, NY 11040
(516) 535-2010
www.squareonepublishers.com

Library of Congress Cataloging-in-Publication Data

Doyle, Arthur Conan, Sir, 1859–1930.
The new revelation: my personal investigation of spiritualism / Arthur Conan Doyle.
p. cm. — (Square One Classics)
Originally published: New York : G.H. Doran, c1918. With new introd.
Includes index.
ISBN 0-7570-0017-7 (pbk.)
1. Spiritualism. I. Title. II. Series.
BF1272 .D7 2001
133.9—dc21

2001001427

Square One Classics is an imprint of Square One Publishers, Inc.

Copyright © 2001 by Square One Publishers

All rights reserved. No part of this publication may be reproduced, stored in a retrieval system, or transmitted, in any form or by any means, electronic, mechanical, photocopying, recording, or otherwise, without the prior written permission of the copyright owner.

Printed in the United States of America

10 9 8 7 6 5 4 3 2 1

Contents

To all the brave men and women,
humble or learned,
who have had the moral courage
during seventy years
to face ridicule or worldly disadvantage
in order to testify
to an all-important truth

Arthur Conan Doyle

MARCH, 1918

Introduction

From 1914–1918 Europeans fought "The Great War," a conflict that would reshape and determine the course of the twentieth century. The assassination of an Austrian archduke had plunged the world into war in 1914, and ensuing years of carnage destroyed the youth of an entire continent. The horrors of trench warfare and the lethal domination of the machine gun caused millions of casualties, and the continuing tragedy drained hope from the population. In a forlorn effort to break the stalemate, the British Army launched a massive attack along the Somme River on July 1, 1916; over 100,000 men assaulted German positions beginning at 7:30 AM, and ten hours later 58,000 of them were casualties. The war seemed endless, all sacrifices meaningless, and people everywhere were nearing the verge of despair.

It was in this year of suffering and questioning that Sir

Arthur Conan Doyle (1859–1930), one of the world's preeminent literary figures, first proclaimed his personal beliefs in Spiritualism, a much-maligned and terribly misunderstood movement whose origins arose in a far-distant past. Doyle believed that Spiritualism, which he had studied for almost three decades, could provide meaning and hope in a violent and cruel world. Although he recognized that Spiritualism was often libeled as a haven for charlatans and fakes, Doyle had become convinced that its principles were both reasonable and susceptible to proof; he knew it brought him solace in terrible times, and he believed that others would find comfort in its practices. But Doyle's personal affirmation hardly dissipated the gloom of the era, and the author soon decided that he had the obligation to provide Englishmen with a strong analysis of the Spiritualist position. *The New Revelation,* published in March 1918, was the result. The reception for his book greatly pleased Doyle, and during the next decade, its message of a serene but fulfilling life after death was identified with the writer to almost the same degree as his earlier literary creation, Sherlock Holmes.

For the next decade, Doyle became the primary spokesman for Spiritualism, a role he considered a far greater importance than writing detective stories. Sir Arthur was fully aware that many considered Spiritualism to be fraudulent, and his dedication of *The New Revelation* clearly recognizes that his popularizing task was a daunting one. In it, Doyle praises "all the brave men and women" who for seventy years had steadfastly upheld different beliefs "in order to testify to an all-important truth." Explicating that truth to a skeptical world was the task Doyle faced as he wrote *The New Revelation*.

Many forces combined to create the Spiritualist movement. Cultures around the world have long believed in "spirit healing," the materialization of the dead, clairvoyance, and the possibility of communication with those who have passed from this earth. European history during the Middle Ages recorded many instances of such strange events as levitation and the hearing of voices—phenomena normally attributed to religious inspiration. Spiritualism's roots also show the influence of Emanuel Swedenborg (1688–1772), a Swedish scientist and equally great mystic. Swedenborg often entered a trance-like state, reviving with information of a religious—and often practical—nature. Franz Mesmer (1734–1815) discovered that placing ordinary individuals into a hypnotic trance could often evoke totally unsuspected powers, insights sometimes useful in the treatment of disease. Nineteenth-century followers of both of these visionaries found it easy to accept the ideas of communication with dead souls through the vehicle of a medium.

But Spiritualism derived its greatest impetus from events that took place in Hydesville, New York, during the mid 1800s—about seventy years before Doyle's publication of *The New Revelation*. During this time, successive occupants of a farmhouse there claimed that it was haunted because they heard unexplained noises in the night. In 1848, a teenage girl, Kate Fox, claimed that she was able to communicate with the source of the sounds, a long-dead peddler who had been murdered in the house. Hydesville was located in the "Burnt-over District," a part of western New York particularly given to religious revivalism. At first, many considered Kate Fox to be merely another indication of excess enthusiasm. But Kate, soon joined by her younger sisters, proved far more than a passing fancy. For the next forty years, they traveled the nation, presiding over séances, and communicating with the dead by means of messages that were delivered by rapping or knocking sounds.

Belief in Spiritualism soared and soon crossed the ocean to Great Britain, where it won support from many prominent men, including essayist John Ruskin and William Wallace, one of Darwin's contemporaries. By the 1880s, attempts to contact departed loved ones were common occurrences in Victorian parlors. It was through such "table-turnings," séances of the grieving or the believing, that Arthur Conan Doyle first encountered Spiritualism. He was then only a provincial doctor, one barely making a living, but he was destined to become a best-loved author. Examining his long, successful, and fascinating life helps us understand why his endorsement of Spiritualism made such an impact on the British nation.

DOYLE'S LIFE

Family heritage helps determine the man, and the Doyles were the product of Ireland. The mystical and magical themes of Irish history were deeply interwoven into the Doyle pedigree; his mother, Mary Foley, could trace her ancestry back to the royal house of the Plantagenets, and his father's family drew deep on the artistic traditions of the island. John Doyle, Arthur's grandfather, won fame in London during the 1830s as the political caricaturist HB, but his father, Charles Altamont, was less gifted. He worked as a civil servant in Edinburgh, the city where he married Mary Foley in July 1855. Their family ultimately numbered ten children, seven of whom lived to maturity; Arthur Conan, the eldest son, was born in Edinburgh on May 22, 1859.

As the young boy grew, he saw how his father's weak nature, his abuse of alcohol, and his increasing epilepsy, caused the family to suffer privation. He watched his mother struggle to keep the household functioning when his father's instability caused his dismissal from the Office of Public Works. Often help came from Charles' concerned brothers, but young Arthur was forced to shoulder responsibility at far too early an age. Yet another source of tension was the family's staunch Roman Catholicism in a Presbyterian world. Arthur was enrolled at the Jesuit preparatory school of Hodder in 1868, and entered Stonyhurst secondary school two years afterwards. A strong-minded but diligent student, Arthur received a first-class education from the Jesuits, even as his mother struggled to pay his tuition bills. Sometime before graduation in 1875, he decided to leave the Church, and, in a way, would spend his life searching for a new faith.

During his school years, Doyle read widely, especially fascinated by the new vision of the natural world presented in the works of Charles Darwin, Herbert Spencer, and Thomas Huxley. Impatient with the credos of religious faith, and repulsed by the dogma that there could be no salvation outside the Church, Doyle particularly devoured Dr. Huxley's writings. He emulated his mentor by proclaiming himself an agnostic, believing in the possibility God, but denying that there can be proof of God's existence. In his autobiography, *Memories and Adventures,* Doyle wrote that "all Christianity, and not Roman Catholicism alone . . . alienated my mind and drives me to agnosticism." Like many authors, Doyle later recounted his personal loss of faith in writing the semi-biographical novel, *The Stark-Munro Letters.* Yet despite his renunciation of Catholicism, Doyle's Jesuit training continued for another year at Feldkirch, in Austria, before he began medical studies at Edinburgh (October 1876).

Five years of study lay before Doyle, a period in which he found the models for both Sherlock Holmes (Dr. Joseph Bell) and Professor George Edward Challenger (Dr. Rutherford) among his professors. No time was wasted, and the young man served as a surgeon's clerk and took several medical assistantships to help pay his way; he also contributed to his mother's household. In September 1879, Doyle published both his first fiction, which appeared in *Chamber's Journal* and for which he received the equivalent of $15.75, and his first medical article, which appeared in the *British Medical Journal.*

Yet the young man longed for adventure, and he left Edinburgh for a term to be surgeon on the Greenland whaler *Hope* from February to September 1880. Much later Doyle happily recalled a "strange and fascinating chapter of life," yet he remained a confirmed landlubber who fell into the ocean so often the crew christened him the "great northern diver." Returning to finish his studies in 1881, he graduated with "fair but not notable distinction" in August 1881. Still lured by the sea, Doyle accepted a three-month posting as ship's doctor on the steamer *Mayumba,* which traveled to West Africa (October 1881). He returned invigorated, yet pronounced the voyage his last. Family responsibilities could not be ignored.

During the 1880s, Dr. Arthur Conan Doyle struggled to choose a life's path. *Memories and Adventures* claims he lived on only a shilling a day during his years of apprenticeship, which began with an ill-fated partnership in Plymouth. Every experience held potential gain, however, he later lampooned his eccentric partner's habits in the *Stark-Munro Letters.* The young doctor relocated to Southsea near Portsmouth in July 1882, and spent the next eight years there in general practice. After his father was institutionalized and his mother had resettled in Yorkshire, Doyle brought his young brother Innes into his home, and the two became inseparable.

Doyle's practice remained small—he never made more than 300 pounds in any year—and he used the frequent quiet periods to write short stories for pocket money. More importantly, in August 1885, he married Louise Hawkins, whom he affectionately nicknamed "Touie," and whose brother had suffered from cerebral meningitis and tragically died under Doyle's care. The happy couple traveled to Ireland on their honeymoon, and when they returned, found that Edinburgh had awarded Doyle an MD degree. With the confidence of youth—Doyle was only twenty-six years old—they faced the future together.

During these lean years, some experts suspect that Doyle could have used his family's strong Roman Catholic connections to increase his practice, but he refused to do so since he had left the Church. Instead, early in 1886, he began work on his first Sherlock Holmes adventure, *A Study in Scarlet.* He had some trouble deciding on the name for his protagonist, and it is interesting to note that Oliver Wendell Holmes—a poet much admired by Doyle—began a speaking tour of Great Britain that summer. After being several times rejected, the novel was finally sold for twenty-five pounds and appeared in *Beeton's Christmas Annual* for 1887. Doyle's future was still uncertain, but the successful debut of Sherlock Holmes marked the beginning of a literary career that would bring him more riches and fame than he could imagine.

In 1886, the year in which Doyle's fertile imagination developed the character of Sherlock Holmes, the young doctor began to read extensively about Spiritualism for the first time. He was a man of science, a seeker of truth who had discarded the faith of his youth and believed himself to be a "convinced materialist." Yet, he was strangely drawn to participate in the "table turnings" that had become fashionable in many parts of Great Britain. He found séances personally fulfilling and attended hundreds of them, including several held by the Scot Daniel Douglas Home. At the time, Home was perhaps the most famous mystic in the British Isles, and some of his manifestations, including a levitation over seventy feet in the air, have never been explained.

As early as July 2, 1887, Doyle defended psychic séances in a letter to the publication *Light.* In addition, he and an architect friend personally conducted a series of experiments in thought transference, which he believed were successful. Convinced that transference of ideas and concepts was possible for some humans, Doyle was inclined to believe that messages from the world of the dead could be similarly sent and received. Besides attending séances, where he took copious notes on the various occurrences, Doyle began to collect books on Spiritualism and ultimately amassed an extensive library. He found comfort in knowing that other prominent scientists "believed that spirit was independent of matter and could survive it." But his growing enthusiasm was blunted by the poor results gained by some mediums and their sometimes obvious manipulations.

In October 1888, Margaret Fox, one of the sisters who stimulated the modern Spiritualist movement, publicly admitted that her family had perpetrated a huge hoax on the public. "Spiritualism is a fraud and a deception," she said, "It is a bunch of legerdemain . . ." Later, both she and her sister Kate would recant their admission, but the blow to believers was, nevertheless, quite substantial. At that time, Doyle was hardly an advocate of the movement, although he was certain there was "an occult influence connecting us with an invisible world." Faced with the need to make a living, he temporarily set aside pursuing his interest in Spiritualism. He did, however, continue to attend séances, even defending Spiritualism in a letter to the *Portsmouth Evening News* (May 1889), but he concentrated most of his abundant energy on building a secure place in a more tangible world. He also joined the recently created Society of Psychical Research (1882), which investigated the claims of psychics and mystics.

The modest success of *A Study in Scarlet* encouraged Doyle to write *Micah Clarke* (1889), his historical novel of the Monmouth Rebellion of 1685. His effort won an immediate audience and the struggling physician suddenly perceived an alternate avenue to wealth and fame, one that would force a choice between his profession and his avocation. To encourage his writing, the American editor of *Lippincott's Magazine* traveled to Britain to solicit another Holmes novel. At a luncheon meeting in London, surely one of the best investments in publishing history, he obtained Doyle's agreement to write *The Sign of the Four,* and convinced another author, Oscar Wilde, to embark on a project that produced *The Picture of Dorian Gray.* Holmes' reappearance in America early in 1890 initiated a vogue for Doyle that has continued beyond the millennium.

Yet Doyle, at the age of thirty, remained unsure about his literary prospects. Uprooting his family, which now included baby Mary (1889), he departed for Vienna to begin study in ophthalmology. Returning in the spring of 1891, he established a London practice on Upper Wimpole Street. But lack of patients deemed the experiment a disaster. Whether it was his brusque manner, or simply Doyle's competition on Harley Street is immaterial. His medical income fell, and scribbling stories became more vital. Fortunately, a new magazine, *The Strand,* had just begun to publish and needed an attraction to build a loyal readership. Mutual need led *The Strand* to publish its first Sherlock Holmes story, "A Scandal in Bohemia," in July 1891. Five others quickly followed, and by the end of the year, Sherlock Holmes had become a publishing phenomenon in Great Britain. Building "The Canon" of four novels and fifty-six Sherlock Holmes adventures was one of Doyle's notable literary accomplishments.

Suddenly, a failed ophthalmologist was a prominent author, and the decision to abandon his practice was inevitable. Although contracted for another six Holmes stories, Doyle's ambition was far larger. As early as November 1891, he wrote his mother Mary that the detective distracted his mind; "I think of slaying Holmes." Doyle was increasingly drawn to what he called "the dream of history," and was elated when his long novel about the Thirty Years War received strong reviews. Some critics consider *The White Company* to be Doyle's masterpiece, and it has never been out of print since its first publication in 1891. Six additional Holmes "adventures" appeared during the first half of 1892 along with a raft of other stories, and Doyle knew his future course was set. Although he received an average of only $175 for each episode, popular acclaim raised the price to $250 by the end of the year. The birth of a first son, Alleyne Kingsley (1892), only completed his contentment. Suddenly in demand, he agreed to co-write a play with his friend James Barrie, but the project failed in 1893. Little more than a decade later, Barrie would bring Peter Pan and Tinker Bell to an enchanted world.

The glories of Doyle's literary output are best assessed by others, but his imaginative abilities seemed endless. He offered a demanding public its choice of historical, medical, or science-fiction stories. His interest in history plundered the Regency, Napoleonic Europe, and the Middle Ages for interesting story lines. While vacationing in Switzerland in 1893, he not only found the place to kill off Holmes, but also discovered the wonders of the ski slope; his travel essays secured the future of Davos as a resort community. After his attempt to kill Holmes failed, and he was forced to revive his creation in 1900, Doyle received $5,000 for every story that was published in the United States. His flow of words for an appreciative audience continued unabated until the time of the Great War.

Only within the heart of his family did Doyle experience sadness. His beloved wife, Touie, had been diagnosed with tuberculosis, and all efforts were directed to easing her suffering. Late in 1895, the couple journeyed to Egypt in order to avoid England's harsh winter and to provide Touie with a dry climate to cure her cough. Doyle also used the trip to accumulate materials for later novels, and, after fighting broke out with the Dervishes, he became a war correspondent, reporting on General Kitchener for the *Westminster Gazette*. The Doyles then returned to a new home built in Surrey, whose fresh breezes were thought able to cure even the frailest of invalids.

Doyle continued to seek information in séances, and was angered when the Catholic Church issued a decree in 1898 that condemned Spiritualism. His writing continued to be successful, and in 1899, he and the actor William Gillette brought Holmes to the stage in a play that provided them both with steady income for thirty years. But the increasing frailty of his wife continued to preoccupy the prolific author.

For his entire life, Doyle was a patriot and defender of the British Empire. Too old to serve in the military during the Boer War, he voluntarily joined a hospital that was sent to the front, and he ministered to the wounded. Recalling the town in which his hospital functioned, Doyle wrote that "you could smell Bloemfontein long before you could see it." As criticism of Great Britain increased, Doyle returned to England to unsuccessfully stand for Parliament as a supporter of the conflict. He wrote a spirited defense of *The War in South Africa; Its Causes and Conduct,* which later was expanded into *The Great Boer War.* For his staunch patriotism, as well as the pleasure his writings had given the world, Arthur Conan Doyle was knighted by King Edward in 1902. He was at first reluctant to accept, but the huge literary success of *The Hound of the Baskervilles* virtually ensured his acquiescence. The next year, a thirteen-volume edition of his works was published in the United States where his reputation was pristine.

In 1906, Touie's long struggle with disease ended, and Doyle entered a bleak period of mourning. Gradually he came to accept his loss, and threw himself into clearing the name of George Edalji, who had been victimized by the legal system. Always willing to embark on such personal crusades, Sir Arthur would later defend a Jew accused of murder, denounce King Leopold for Belgium's actions in the Congo, serve as president of the Divorce Law Reform Union, campaign for a "chunnel," and fight for Irish home rule. The author also found comfort in his friendship with Jean Leckie, a woman he had first met in 1897 and who had helped him cope with Touie's illness. Doyle's personal recovery was signaled when, after consulting with his children, he married Jean on September 18, 1907. Their union produced the additional children both desired, and the couple would soon share a belief in Spiritualism as well. The Doyles soon moved to a new home, Windlesham, in Crow borough, and happily remained there for the rest of their marriage.

Holmes stories continued to appear at intervals to the delight of Doyle's readers. But in the years before the Great War, Doyle was able to create a new hero—Professor Edward Challenger—whose adventures in *The Lost World* (1912) and *The Poison Belt* (1913) briefly competed for public favor with Doyle's famous detective. It is perhaps significant that in contrast to the ever-rational Holmes, Challenger's scientific mind found it possible to accept things beyond the understanding of modern thought.

THE NEW REVELATION

With the outbreak of the Great War, Doyle once again dreamed of active service, but his age limited the author to organizing local forces that were ultimately consolidated into the Sixth Royal Sussex Volunteer's. More importantly, during 1914, Jean's bridesmaid and oldest friend, Lily Lodes-Symonds, joined the household as a nanny for the children. She soon fell ill, perhaps in reaction to the loss of her brother during the battle of Mons, but stayed on as a member of the family. While bedridden, Lily suddenly developed an unexpected ability to receive messages from beyond the grave and communicate them through "automatic writing." Sir Arthur had seen many such cases in which spirits communicated their messages to the living through the mechanism of a medium's hand, but never as personally as with Lily. Such messages always raise the question of origin; do they arise from a spirit, the subconscious mind of the medium, or simply from fakery? Doyle reported that Lily's ability to convey messages was sometimes notable only for its errors, so he was absolutely astonished when Lily accurately recounted a private conversation he had held with Jean's brother Malcolm (also a war victim).

The incident became Doyle's "moment of truth." His long search for a personal faith was over, and Doyle's personal manifesto of belief appeared in *Light* (November 4, 1916). Spiritualism, which he had studied since 1887, is closer to "Truth" than any existing creed, and it can be "the foundation of a definite system of religious thought." It is "confirmitory of ancient systems," yet new and fulfilling on its own terms. At the end of 1916, Sir Arthur decided that he would personally devote the rest of his life to publicizing Spiritualism, a movement offering "hope and guidance to the human race at the time of its deepest affliction."

In the meantime, the Great War continued to inflict its terrible toll on Europe. Doyle's literary prominence earned him a battlefront tour of three fronts, and his pen quickly began to produce reports, which became *The British Campaign in France and Flanders.* His cogent dispatches appeared throughout World War I, sometimes interrupted by censors, and were the basis for a six-volume history, which appeared in 1920. The author's lively social conscience led him also to protest the treatment of the leaders of the Easter Rising in Dublin (1916) and the execution of Sir Roger Casement. All the while he was mulling over his course regarding Spiritualism, and on October 17, 1917, he spoke to the London Spiritualist Society on what he called "The New Revelation." Sir Arthur's talk became the basis for his larger, more organized book, which appeared the following March.

The New Revelation offers a sustained plea for the understanding and recognition of Spiritualism as a major force. It must be remembered that Sir Arthur was a trained scientist, a skilled observer who was famed for his logical mind. These attributes had brought him fame and vast wealth, but no personal fulfillment. For decades he had studied the phenomena of Spiritualism without making a final commitment, but his experience with Lily ended his doubts. Spiritualism was a belief that could be verified, it could satisfy the demands of his modern mind and provide comfort. Life was a continuum, a progression into ever-greater knowledge and understanding that linked the souls of all people. *The New Revelation* explained his views and became the most influential statement of the movement. It represents Doyle's most mature judgment, for it was written and published long before the war brought personal tragedy to his household. Later in 1918, Lily passed away, and then Doyle's eldest son, Kingsley, died from a case of influenza. Equally tragic was the death of his beloved brother Brigadier General Innes Doyle, who succumbed to pneumonia in 1919.

The tragic deaths of two of his closest relatives did not force Doyle towards Spiritualism as a means of solace. Reason and experience had convinced him that there was life after death, and that some gifted people could make a connection between the two worlds. While professing the greatest respect for the ideals of Christ, Mohammed, and the Buddha, Doyle focused all his personal efforts on clarifying the meaning of Spiritualism and how it might be of benefit to everyone.

The New Revelation was quickly followed by *The Vital Message* (1919), and many English families who had lost loved ones during the war readily listened to this new gospel of hope. Both volumes became steady sellers, and for the remaining years of his life, Doyle would become the greatest proponent of Spiritualism both as writer and lecturer. Belief in the paranormal became the driving force of his life, and, no matter how often mediums were exposed as frauds, his faith never faltered. Moreover, his public support for mediums who were able to channel with the dead intensified. In 1919, he endorsed a Welsh medium who had established a connection with his dead son, a true revelation since during the séance, the son's spirit "spoke of concerns unknown to the medium." Other mediums brought Doyle into the presence of his mother and dead brother. In fact, by 1920, Doyle claimed to have established communication twice with Innes and six times with Kingsley.

In the 1920s, Sir Arthur toured the globe preaching the "new revelation" in which he put his faith. His travels took him to Australia, South Africa, North America, and to every part of Europe. He seemed particularly pleased with the two trips he made to the United States and Canada (1922–1923), during which he resumed his acquaintance with the renowned magician Harry Houdini (1874–1926). Both men were intensely interested in Spiritualism, but Houdini's skepticism ultimately would cause a break in their friendship. Through a series of excerpted letters, their relationship is detailed in this book's Afterword, beginning on page 97.

Sir Arthur was a gifted speaker, a friendly father figure who quickly established a relationship with his audience. His talent included the ability to speak with, not down to, the people who had come both to see the creator of Sherlock Holmes and Edward Challenger and to seek spiritual consolation. Wherever he appeared, crowds flocked to hear Doyle speak of his experiences. He told audiences that love, interests, and even hobbies survived death, and that souls with now perfect bodies enjoyed marriage with ideal mates. Both alcohol and tobacco use continued in the world of the dead, but sexual activity was no longer necessary. In the course of his standard lecture, Doyle always cautioned that some mediums were frauds, but contended that even true mediums could experience difficulties in establishing contact with the other side. Ruefully he also admitted that some true mediums cheated when their powers failed. But he held "no question of the validity of the Spiritualist experience," and documented it with slides, photos, and personal testimony. "If it were only a matter of faith," said Doyle, "then I might as well go back to the faith of my fathers." Despite Doyle's fervent proselytizing, his American tours were more successful financially than they were in gaining converts. This enabled the author to donate substantial sums to Spiritualist causes. He returned to Great Britain in 1923.

As Spiritualism's greatest defender, books and pamphlets continued to flow from his ever-ready arsenal of words—his dozen books on the subject include *Spiritualism and Rationalism, Wanderings of a Spiritualist, The Case for Psychic Photography, The Coming of the Fairies,* and his autobiography, *Memories and Adventures.* Doyle chronicled his North American "adventure" in two volumes, which enjoyed substantial sales. Regarding the survival of Spiritualism itself, he personally held no doubts.

During the last years of his long and extraordinarily productive life, Doyle continued to tour and to write. In 1925, he financed the Psychic Bookshop, Library and Museum in London, but it proved to be an expensive failure. He took comfort from the fact that he had achieved communication with an individual spirit guide named Pheneas, an Arabian who had lived in Ur, whose messages Doyle gave to the world in 1927. His literary concerns were now almost exclusively devoted to Spiritualism, and he published a major history of the movement while rebutting attacks on its tenets. In a tape recording that still exists, he affirms that Spiritualism had provided him with serenity, it "absolutely removes all fear of death," and readies one to meet God. No medium's failure to communicate, no exposure of fraud disturbed his confidence that there was another side. Whether or not spirits came was unimportant, "they come if they wish and the initiative is always with them," and they follow the will of God in their appearances. A film made by the Movietone News (1929) shows a dignified, even youthful-looking Sir Arthur eager to share his faith. He considered himself a missionary, one who happened to be a public figure able to inform "less fortunate" people there is real hope. "I'm not talking about what I believe, I'm talking about what I know."

After touring Scandinavia late in 1929, Doyle, at age seventy, returned to London with a severe case of angina. In spite of his failing health, he continued to fight Spiritualism's battles, responding to an attack by H.G. Wells, and resigning from the Society of Psychical Research in 1930 to protest its refusal to accept séance insights. But doctors could not reverse his decline, and Sir Arthur Conan Doyle died at 9:30 AM on July 7, 1930. The news sped across the ocean, and the New York *World* announced his death with an epitaph Doyle would have loved. Beneath a photo of the renowned author was the caption, "His Greatest Adventure."

As Great Britain and the world mourned, Doyle was buried near his summerhouse at Windlesham. On July 13, during a memorial service in Albert Hall, several mediums affirmed that Sir Arthur in full evening dress sat in the empty chair next to his grieving widow. It is a matter of record that Lady Doyle asserted the family achieved communication with him before the end of the month. Some may dispute her claim, but all agreed with the epitaph she placed on his gravestone: Steel True, Blade Straight.

George J. Lankevich, PhD
Historian, Author

The New Revelation

CHAPTER I

The Search

THE SUBJECT OF PSYCHICAL RESEARCH is one upon which I have thought more and about which I have been slower to form my opinion, than upon any other subject whatever. Every now and then as one jogs along through life some small incident happens which very forcibly brings home the fact that time passes and that first youth and then middle age are slipping away. Such a one occurred the other day. There is a column in that excellent little paper, *Light,* which is devoted to what was recorded on the corresponding date a generation—that is thirty years—ago. As I read over this column recently I had quite a start as I saw my own name, and read the reprint of a letter which I had written in 1887, detailing some interesting spiritual experience which had occurred in a séance. Thus it is manifest that my interest in the subject is of some standing, and also, since it is only within the last year or two that I have finally declared myself to be satisfied with the evidence, that I have not been hasty in forming my opinion. If I had set down some of my experiences and difficulties my readers will not, I hope, think it egotistical upon my part, but will realise that it is the most graphic way in which to sketch out the points which are likely to occur to any other inquirer. When I have passed over this ground, it will be possible to get on to something more general and impersonal in its nature.

When I had finished my medical education in 1882, I found myself, like many young medical men, a convinced Materialist as regards our personal destiny. I had never ceased to be an earnest theist, because it seemed to me that Napoleon's question to the atheistic professors on the starry night as he voyaged to Egypt: "Who was it, gentlemen, who made these stars?" has never been answered. To say that the Universe was made by immutable laws only put the question one degree further back as to who made the laws. I did not, of course, believe in an anthropomorphic God, but I believed then, as I believe now, in an intelligent Force behind all the operations of Nature—a force so infinitely complex and great that my finite brain could get no further than its existence. Right and wrong I saw also as great obvious facts which needed no divine revelation. But when it came to a question of our little personalities surviving death, it seemed to me that the whole analogy of Nature was against it. When the candle burns out the light disappears. When the electric cell is shattered the current stops. When the body dissolves there is an end of the matter. Each man in his egotism may feel that he ought to survive, but let him look, we will say, at the average loafer—of high or low degree—would anyone contend that there was any obvious reason why *that* personality should carry on? It seemed to be a delusion, and I was convinced that death did indeed end all, though I saw no reason why that should affect our duty towards humanity during our transitory existence.

This was my frame of mind when spiritual phenomena first came before my notice. I had always regarded the subject as the greatest nonsense upon earth, and I had read of the conviction of fraudulent mediums and wondered how any sane man could believe such things. I met some friends, however, who were interested in the matter, and I sat with them at some table-moving séances. We got connected messages. I am afraid the only result that they had on my mind was that I regarded these friends with some suspicion. They were long messages very often, spelled out by tilts, and it was quite impossible that they came by chance. Someone then, was moving the table. I thought it was they. They probably thought that I did it. I was puzzled and worried over it, for they were not people whom I could imagine as cheating—and yet I could not see how the messages could come except by conscious pressure.

About this time—it would be in 1886—I came across a book called *The Reminiscences of Judge Edmunds.* He was a judge of the U.S. High Courts and a man of high standing. The book gave an account of how his wife had died, and how he had been able for many years to keep in touch with her. All sorts of details were given. I read the book with interest, and absolute scepticism. It seemed to me an example of how a hard practical man might have a weak side to his brain, a sort of reaction, as it were, against those plain facts of life with which he had to deal. Where was this spirit of which he talked? Suppose a man had an accident and cracked his skull; his whole character would change, and a high nature might become a low one. With alcohol or opium or many other drugs one could apparently quite change a man's spirit. The spirit then depended upon matter. These were the arguments which I used in those days. I did not realise that it was not the spirit that was changed in such cases, but the body through which the spirit worked, just as it would be no argument against the existence of a musician if you tampered with his violin so that only discordant notes could come through.

I was sufficiently interested to continue to read such literature as came in my way. I was amazed to find what a number of great men—men whose names were to the fore in science—thoroughly believed that spirit was independent of matter and could survive it. When I regarded Spiritualism as a vulgar delusion of the uneducated, I could afford to look down upon it; but when it was endorsed by men like Crookes, whom I knew to be the most rising British chemist, by Wallace, who was the rival of Darwin, and by Flammarion, the best known of astronomers, I could not afford to dismiss it. It was all very well to throw down the books of these men which contained their mature conclusions and careful investigations, and to say "Well, he has one weak spot in his brain," but a man has to be very self-satisfied if the day does not come when he wonders if the weak spot is not in his own brain. For some time I was sustained in my scepticism by the consideration that many famous men, such as Darwin himself, Huxley, Tyndall and Herbert Spencer, decided this new branch of knowledge; but when I learned that their derision had reached such a point that they would not even examine it, and that Spencer had declared in so many words that he had decided against it on *a priori* [deductive] grounds, while Huxley had said that it did not interest him, I was bound to admit that, however great they were in Science, their action in this respect was most unscientific and dogmatic, while the action of those who studied the phenomena and tried to find out the laws that governed them, was following the true path which has given us all human advance and knowledge. So far I had got in my reasoning, so my sceptical position was not so solid as before.

It was somewhat reinforced, however, by my own experiences. It is to be remembered that I was working without a medium, which is like an astronomer working without a telescope. I have no psychical powers myself, and those who worked with me had little more. Among us we could just muster enough of the magnetic force, or whatever you will call it, to get the table movements with their suspicious and often stupid messages. I still have notes of those sittings and copies of some, at least, of the messages. They were not always absolutely stupid. For example, I find that on one occasion, on my asking some test question, such as how many coins I had in my pocket, the table spelt out: "We are here to educate and to elevate, not to guess riddles." And then: "The religious frame of mind, not the critical, is what we wish to inculcate." Now, no one could say that that was a puerile message. On the other hand, I was always haunted by the fear of involuntary pressure from the hands of the sitters. Then there came an incident which puzzled and disgusted me very much. We had very good conditions one evening, and an amount of movement which seemed quite independent of our pressure. Long and detailed messages came through, which purported to be from a spirit who gave his name and said he was a commercial traveller who had lost his life in a recent fire at a theatre at Exeter. All the details were exact, and he implored us to write to his family, who lived, he said, at a place called Slattenmere, in Cumberland. I did so, but my letter came back, appropriately enough, through the dead letter office. To this day I do not know whether we were deceived, or whether there was some mistake in the name of the place; but there are the facts, and I was so disgusted that for some time my interest in the whole subject waned. It was one thing to study a subject, but when the subject began to play elaborate practical jokes it seemed time to call a halt. If there is such a place as Slattenmere in the world I should even now be glad to know it.

I was in practice in Southsea at this time, and dwelling there was General Drayson, a man of very remarkable character, and one of the pioneers of Spiritualism in this country. To him I went with my difficulties, and he listened to them very patiently. He made light of my criticism of the foolish nature of many of these messages, and of the absolute falseness of some. "You have not got the fundamental truth into your head," said he. "That truth is, that every spirit in the flesh passes over to the next world exactly as it is, with no change whatever. This world is full of weak or foolish people. So is the next. You need not mix with them, any more than you do in this world. One chooses one's companions. But suppose a man in this world, who had lived in his house alone and never mixed with his fellows, was at last to put his head out of the window to see what sort of place it was, what would happen? Some naughty boy would probably say something rude. Anyhow, he would see nothing of the wisdom or greatness of the world. He would draw his head in thinking it was a very poor place. That is just what you have done. In a mixed séance, with no definite aim, you have thrust your head into the next world and you have met some naughty boys. Go forward and try to reach something better." That was General Drayson's explanation, and though it did not satisfy me at the time, I think now that it was a rough approximation to the truth.

These were my first steps in Spiritualism. I was still a sceptic, but at least I was an inquirer, and when I heard some old-fashioned critic saying that there was nothing to explain, and that it was all fraud, or that a conjuror was needed to show it up, I knew at least that that was all nonsense. It is true that my own evidence up to then was not enough to convince me, but my reading, which was continuous, showed me how deeply other men had gone into it, and I recognised that the testimony was so strong that no other religious movement in the world could put forward anything to compare with it. That did not prove it to be true, but at least it proved that it must be treated with respect and could not be brushed aside. Take a single incident of what Wallace has truly called a modern miracle. I choose it because it is the most incredible. I allude to the assertion that D.D. Home—who, by the way, was not, as is usually supposed, a paid adventurer, but was the nephew of the Earl of Home—the assertion, I say, that he floated out of one window and into another at the height of seventy feet above the ground. I could not believe it. And yet, when I knew that the fact was attested by three eye-witnesses, who were Lord Dunraven, Lord Lindsay, and Captain Wynne, all men of honour and repute, who were willing afterwards to take their oath upon it, I could not but admit that the evidence for this was more direct than for any of those far-off events which the whole world has agreed to accept as true.

I still continued during these years to hold table séances, which sometimes gave no results, sometimes trivial ones, and sometimes rather surprising ones. I have still the notes of these sittings, and I extract here the results of one which were definite, and which were so unlike any conceptions which I held of life beyond the grave that they amused rather than edified me at the time. I find now, however, that they agree very closely with the revelations in *Raymond* [by Oliver Lodge] and in other later accounts, so that I view them with different eyes.

I am aware that all these accounts of life beyond the grave differ in detail—I suppose any of our accounts of the present life would differ in detail—but in the main there is a very great resemblance, which in this instance was very far from the conception either of myself or of either of the two ladies who made up the circle. Two communicators sent messages, the first of whom spelt out as a name "Dorothy Pothlewaite," a name unknown to any of us. She said she died at Melbourne five years before, at the age of sixteen, that she was now happy, that she had work to do, and that she had been at the same school as one of the ladies. On my asking that lady to raise her hands and give a succession of names, the table tilted at the correct name of the head mistress of the school. This seemed in the nature of a test. She went on to say that the sphere she inhabited was all round the earth; that she knew about the planets; that Mars was inhabited by a race more advanced than us, and that the canals were artificial; there was no bodily pain in her sphere, but there could be mental anxiety; they were governed; they took nourishment; she had been a Catholic and was still a Catholic, but had not fared better than the Protestants; there were Buddhists and Mohammedans in her sphere, but all fared alike; she had never seen Christ and knew no more about Him than on earth, but believed in His influence; spirits prayed and they died in their new sphere before entering another; they had pleasures—music was among them. It was a place of light and of laughter. She added that they had no rich or poor, and that the general conditions were far happier than on earth.

This lady bade us good-night, and immediately the table was seized by a much more robust influence, which dashed it about very violently. In answer to my questions it claimed to be the spirit of one whom I will call Dodd, who was a famous cricketer, and with whom I had some serious conversation in

Cairo before he went up the Nile, where he met his death in the Dongolese Expedition. We have now, I may remark, come to the year 1896 in my experiences. Dodd was not known to either lady. I began to ask him questions exactly as if he were seated before me, and he sent his answers back with great speed and decision. The answers were often quite opposed to what I expected, so that I could not believe that I was influencing them. He said that he was happy, that he did not wish to return to earth. He had been a free-thinker, but had not suffered in the next life for that reason. Prayer, however, was a good thing, as keeping us in touch with the spiritual world. If he had prayed more he would have been higher in the spirit world.

This, I may remark, seemed rather in conflict with his assertion that he had not suffered through being a free-thinker, and yet, of course, many men neglect prayer who are not free-thinkers.

His death was painless. He remembered the death of Polwhele, a young officer who died before him. When he (Dodd) died he had found people to welcome him, but Polwhele had not been among them.

He had work to do. He was aware of the Fall of Dolonga, but had not been present in spirit at the banquet at Cairo afterwards. He knew more than he did in life. He remembered our conversation in Cairo. Duration of life in the next sphere was shorter than on earth. He had not seen General Gordon, nor any other famous spirit. Spirits lived in families and in communities. Married people did not necessarily meet again, but those who loved each other did meet again.

I have given this synopsis of a communication to show the kind of thing we got—though this was a very favourable specimen, both for length and for coherence. It shows that it is not just to say, as many critics say, that nothing but folly comes through. There was no folly here unless we call everything folly which does not agree with pre-conceived ideas. On the other hand, what proof was there that these statements were true? I could see no such proof, and they simply left me bewildered. Now, with a larger experience, in which I find that the same sort of information has come to very many people independently in many lands, I think that the agreement of the witnesses does, as in all cases of evidence, constitute some argument for their truth. At the time I could not fit such a conception of the future world into my own scheme of philosophy, and I merely noted it and passed on.

I continued to read many books upon the subject and to appreciate more and more what a cloud of witnesses existed, and how careful their observations had been. This impressed my mind very much more than the limited phenomena which came within the reach of our circle. Then or afterwards I read a book by Monsieur Jacolliot upon occult phenomena in India. Jacolliot was Chief Judge of the French Colony of Crandenagur, with a very judicial mind, but rather biassed against Spiritualism. He conducted a series of experiments with native fakirs, who gave him their confidence because he was a sympathetic man and spoke their language. He describes the pains he took to eliminate fraud. To cut a long story short he found among them every phenomenon of advanced European mediumship, everything which Home, for example, had ever done. He got levitation of the body, the handling of fire, movement of articles at a distance, rapid growth of plants, raising of tables. Their explanation of these phenomena was that they were done by the Pitris or spirits, and their only difference in procedure from ours seemed to be that they made more use of direct evocation. They claimed that these powers were handed down from time immemorial and traced back to the Chaldees. All this impressed me very much, as here, independently, we had exactly the same results, without any question of American frauds, or modern vulgarity, which were so often raised against similar phenomena in Europe.

My mind was also influenced about this time by the report of the Dialectical Society, although this report had been presented as far back as 1869. It is a very cogent paper, and though it was received with a chorus of ridicule by the ignorant and materialistic papers of those days, it was a document of great value. The Society was formed by a number of people of good standing and open mind to enquire into the physical phenomena of Spiritualism. A full account of their experiences and of their elaborate precautions against fraud are given. After reading the evidence, one fails to see how they could have come to any other conclusion than the one attained, namely, that the phenomena were undoubtedly genuine, and that they pointed to laws and forces which had not been explored by Science. It is a most singular fact that if the verdict had been against Spiritualism, it would certainly have been hailed as the death blow of the movement, whereas being an endorsement of the phenomena it met with nothing by ridicule. This has been the fate of a number of inquiries since those conducted locally at Hydesville in 1848, or that which followed when Professor Hare of Philadelphia, like Saint Paul, started forth to oppose but was forced to yield to the truth.

About 1891, I had joined the Society of Psychical Research and had the advantage of reading all their reports. The world owes a great deal to the unwearied diligence of the Society, and to its sobriety of statement, though I will admit that the latter makes one impatient at times, and one feels that in their desire to avoid sensationalism they discourage the world from knowing and using the splendid work which they are doing. Their semi-scientific terminology also chokes off the ordinary reader, and one might say sometimes after reading their articles what an American trapper in the Rocky Mountains said to me about some University man whom he had been escorting for the season. "He was that clever," he said, "that you could not understand what he said." But in spite of these little peculiarities all of us who have wanted light in the darkness have found it by the methodical, never-tiring work of the Society. Its influence was one of the powers which now helped me to shape my thoughts.

There was another, however, which made a deep impression upon me. Up to now I had read all the wonderful experiences of great experimenters, but I had never come across any effort upon their part to build up some system which would cover and contain them all. Now I read that monumental book, Myers' *Human Personality*, a great root book from which a whole tree of knowledge will grow. In this book Myers was unable to get any formula which covered all the phenomena called "spiritual," but in discussing that action of mind upon mind which he has himself called telepathy he completely proved his point, and he worked it out so thoroughly with so many examples, that, save for those who were wilfully blind to the evidence, it took its place henceforth as a scientific fact. But this was an enormous advance. If mind could act upon mind at a distance, then there were some human powers which were quite different to matter as we had always understood it.

The ground was cut from under the feet of the Materialist, and my old position had been destroyed. I had said that the flame could not exist when the candle was gone. But here was the flame a long way off the candle, acting upon its own. The analogy was clearly a false analogy. If the mind, the spirit, the intelligence of man could operate at a distance from the body, then it was a thing to that extent separate from the body. Why then should it not exist on its own when the body was destroyed? Not only did impressions come from a distance in the case of those who were just dead, but the same evidence proved that actual appearances of the dead person came with them, showing that the impressions were carried by something which was exactly like the body, and yet acted independently and survived the death of the body. The chain of evidence between the simplest cases of thought-reading at one end, and the actual manifestation of the spirit independently of the body at the other, was one unbroken chain, each phase leading to the other, and this fact seemed to me to bring the first signs of systematic science and order into what had been a mere collection of bewildering and more or less unrelated facts.

About this time I had an interesting experience, for I was one of three delegates sent by the Psychical Society to sit up in a haunted house. It was one of these poltergeist cases, where noises and foolish tricks had gone on for some years, very much like the classical case of John Wesley's family at Epworth in 1726, or the case of the Fox family at Hydesville near Rochester in 1848, which was the starting-point of modern Spiritualism. Nothing sensational came of our journey, and yet it was not entirely barren. On the first night nothing occurred. On the second, there were tremendous noises, sounds like someone beating a table with a stick. We had, of course, taken every precaution, and we could not explain the noises; but at the same time we could not swear that some ingenious practical joke had not been played upon us. There the matter ended for the time. Some years afterwards, however, I met a member of the family who occupied the house, and he told me that after our visit the bones of a child, evidently long buried, had been dug up in the garden. You must admit that this was very remarkable. Haunted houses are rare, and houses with buried human beings in their gardens are also, we will hope, rare. That they should have both united in one house is surely some argument for the truth of the phenomena. It is interesting to remember that in the case of the Fox family there was also some word of human bones and evidence of murder being found in the cellar, though an actual crime was never established. I have little doubt that if the Wesley family could have got upon speaking terms with their persecutor, they would also have come upon some motive for the persecution. It almost seems as if a life cut suddenly and violently short had some store of unspent vitality which could still manifest itself in a strange, mischievous fashion. Later I had another singular personal experience of this sort which I may describe at the end of this argument. [See "The Cheriton Dugout," pages 39–43.]

From this period until the time of the War, I continued in the leisure hours of a very busy life to devote attention to this subject. I had experience of one series of séances with very amazing results, including several materialisations seen in dim light. As the medium was detected in trickery shortly afterwards I wiped these off entirely as evidence. At the same time I think that the presumption is very clear, that in the case of some mediums like Eusapia Palladino they may be guilty of trickery when their powers fail them, and yet at other times have very genuine gifts. Mediumship in its lowest forms is a purely physical gift with no relation to morality and in many cases it is intermittent and cannot be controlled at will. Eusapia was at least twice convicted of very clumsy and foolish fraud, whereas she several times sustained long examinations under every possible test condition at the hands of scientific committees which contained some of the best names of France, Italy, and England. However, I personally prefer to cut my experience with a discredited medium out of my record, and I think that all physical phenomena produced in the dark must necessarily lose much of

The Cheriton Dugout

I have mentioned in the text that I had some recent experience of a case where a "poltergeist" or mischievous spirit had been manifesting. These entities appear to be of an undeveloped order and nearer to earth conditions than any others with which we are acquainted. This comparative materialism upon their part places them low in the scale of spirit, and undesirable perhaps as communicants, but it gives them a special value as calling attention to crude obvious phenomena, and so arresting the human attention and forcing upon our notice that there are other forms of life within the universe. These borderland forces have attracted passing attention at several times and places in the past, such cases as the Wesley persecution at Epworth, the Drummer of Tedworth, the Bells of Bealing, etc., startling the country for a time—each of them being an impingement of unknown forces upon human life. Then almost simultaneously came the Hydesville case in America and the Cideville disturbances in France, which were so marked that they could not be overlooked. From them sprang the whole modern movement which, reasoning upwards from small things to great, from raw things to developed ones, from phenomena to messages, is destined to give religion the firmest basis upon which it has ever stood. Therefore, humble and foolish as these manifestations may seem, they have been the seed of large developments, and are worthy of our respectful, though critical, attention.

Many such manifestations have appeared of recent years in various quarters of the world, each of which is treated by the press in a more or less comic vein, with a conviction apparently that the use of the word "spook" discredits the incident and brings discussion to an end. It is remarkable that each is treated as an entirely isolated phenomenon, and thus the ordinary reader gets no idea of the strength of the cumulative evidence. In this particular case of the Cheriton Dugout the facts are as follows:

Mr. Jaques, a Justice of the Peace and a man of education and intelligence, residing at Embrook House, Cheriton, near Folkestone, made a dugout just opposite to his residence as a protection against air raids. The house was, it may be remarked, of great antiquity, part of it being an old religious foundation of the 14th Century. The dugout was constructed at the base of a small bluff, and the sinking was through ordinary soft sandstone. The work was carried out by a local jobbing builder called Rolfe, assisted by a lad. Soon after the inception of his task he was annoyed by his candle being continually blown out by jets of sand, and by similar jets hitting up against his own face. These phenomena he imagined to be due to some gaseous or electrical cause, but they reached such a point that his work was seriously hampered, and he complained to Mr. Jaques, who received the story with absolute incredulity. The persecution continued, however, and increased in intensity, taking the form now of actual blows from moving material, considerable objects, such as stones and bits of brick, flying past him and hitting the walls with a violent impact. Mr. Rolfe, still searching for a physical explanation, went to Mr. Hesketh, the Municipal Electrician of Folkestone, a man of high education and intelligence, who went out to the scene of the affair and saw enough to convince himself that the phenomena were perfectly genuine and inexplicable by ordinary laws.

A Canadian soldier who was billeted upon Mr. Rolfe, heard an account of the happenings from his host, and after announcing his conviction that the latter had "bats in his belfry" proceeded to the dugout, where his experiences were so instant and so violent that he rushed out of the place in horror. The housekeeper at the Hall also was a witness of the movement of bricks when no human hands touched them. Mr. Jaques, whose incredulity had gradually thawed before all this evidence, went down to the dugout in the absence of everyone, and was departing from it when five stones rapped up against the door from the inside. He reopened the door and saw them lying there upon the floor. Sir William Barratt had meanwhile come down, but had seen nothing. His stay was a short one.

I afterwards made four visits of about two hours each to the grotto, but got nothing direct, though I saw the new brickwork all chipped about by the blows which it had received. The forces appeared to have not the slightest interest in psychical research, for they never played up to an investigator, and yet their presence and action have been demonstrated to at least seven different observers, and, as I have said, they left their traces behind them, even to the extent of picking the flint stones out of the new cement which was to form the floor, and arranging them in tidy little piles. The obvious explanation that the boy was an adept at mischief had to be set aside in view of the fact that the phenomena occurred in his absence. One extra man of science wandered on to the scene for a moment, but as his explanation was that the movements occurred through the emanation of marsh-gas, it did not advance matters much. The disturbances are still proceeding, and I have had a letter this very morning (February 21st, 1918) with fuller and later details from Mr. Hesketh, the Engineer.

What is the *real* explanation of such a matter? I can only say that I have advised Mr. Jaques to dig into the bluff under which he is constructing his cellar. I made some investigation myself upon the top of it and convinced myself that the surface ground at that spot has at some time been disturbed to the depth of at least five feet. Something has, I should judge, been buried at some date, and it is probable that, as in the case cited in the text, there is a connection between this and the disturbances. It is very probable that Mr. Rolfe is, unknown to himself, a physical medium, and that when he was in the confined space of the cellar he turned it into a cabinet in which his magnetic powers could accumulate and be available for use. It chanced that there was on the spot some agency which chose to use them, and hence the phenomena. When Mr. Jaques went alone to the grotto the power left behind by Mr. Rolfe, who had been in it all morning, was not yet exhausted and he was able to get some manifestations. So I read it, but it is well not to be dogmatic on such matters. If there is systematic digging I should expect an epilogue to the story.

Whilst these proofs were in the press a second very marked case of a poltergeist came within my knowledge. I cannot without breach of confidence reveal the details and the phenomena are still going on. Curiously enough, it was because one of the sufferers from the invasion read some remarks of mine upon the Cheriton Dugout that this other case came to my knowledge, for the lady wrote to me at once for advice and assistance. The place is remote and I have not yet been able to visit it, but from the full accounts which I have now received it seems to present all the familiar features, with the phenomenon of direct writing superadded. Some specimens of this script have reached me. Two clergymen have endeavoured to mitigate the phenomena, which are occasionally very violent, but so far without result. It may be some consolation to any others who may be suffering from this strange infliction, to know that in the many cases which have been carefully recorded there is none in which any physical harm has been inflicted upon man or beast.

their value, unless they are accompanied by evidential messages as well. It is the custom of our critics to assume if you cut out the mediums who got into trouble you would have to cut out nearly all your evidence. That is not so at all. Up to the time of this incident I had never sat with a professional medium at all, and yet I had certainly accumulated some evidence. The greatest medium of all, Mr. D.D. Home, showed his phenomena in broad daylight, and was ready to submit to every test and no charge of trickery was ever substantiated against him. So it was with many others. It is only fair to state in addition that when a public medium is a fair mark for notoriety hunters, for amateur detectives and for sensational reporters, and when he is dealing with obscure elusive phenomena and has to defend himself before juries and judges who, as a rule, know nothing about the conditions which influence the phenomena, it would be wonderful if a man could get through without an occasional scandal. At the same time the whole system of paying by results, which is practically the present system, since if a medium never gets results he would soon get no payments, is a vicious one. It is only when the professional medium can be guaranteed an annuity which will be independent of results, that we can eliminate the strong temptation to substitute pretended phenomena when the real ones are wanting.

I have now traced my own evolution of thought up to the time of the War. I can claim, I hope, that it was deliberate and showed no traces of that credulity with which our opponents charge us. It was too deliberate, for I was culpably slow in throwing any small influence I may possess into the scale of truth. I might have drifted on for my whole life as a psychical researcher, showing a sympathetic, but more or less dilettante attitude towards the whole subject, as if we were arguing about some impersonal thing such as the existence of Atlantis or the Baconian controversy. But the War came, and when the War came it brought earnestness into all our souls and made us look more closely at our own beliefs and reassess their values. In the presence of an agonized world, hearing every day of the deaths of the flower of our race in the first promise of their unfulfilled youth, seeing around one the wives and mothers who had no clear conception whither their loved ones had gone to, I seemed suddenly to see that this subject with which I had so long dallied was not merely a study of a force outside the rules of Science, but that it was really something tremendous, a breaking down of the walls between two worlds, a direct undeniable message from beyond, a call of hope and of guidance to the human race at the time of its deepest affliction. The objective side of it ceased to interest for having made up one's mind that it was true there was an end of the matter. The religious side of it was clearly of infinitely greater importance. The telephone bell in itself a very childish affair, but it may be the signal for a very vital message. It seemed that all these phenomena, large and small, had been the telephone bells which, senseless in themselves, had signalled to the human race: "Rouse yourselves! Stand by! Be at attention! Here are signs for you. They will lead up to the message which God wishes to send." It was the message not the signs which really counted.

A new revelation seemed to be in the course of delivery to the human race, though how far it was still in what may be called the John-the-Baptist stage, and how far some greater fulness and clearness might be expected hereafter, was more than any man can say. My point is, that the physical phenomena which have been proved up to the hilt for all who care to examine the evidence, are really of no account, and that their real value consists in the fact that they support and give objective reality to an immense body of knowledge which must deeply modify our previous religious views, and must, when properly understood and digested, make religion a very real thing, no longer a matter of faith, but a matter of actual experience and fact. It is to this side of the question that I will now turn, but I must add to my previous remarks about personal experience that, since the War, I have had some very exceptional opportunities of confirming all the views which I had already formed as to the truth of the general facts upon which my views are founded.

These opportunities came through the fact that a lady who lived with us, a Miss L.S., developed the power of automatic writing. Of all forms of mediumship, this seems to me to be the one which should be tested most rigidly, as it lends itself very easily not so much to deception as to self-deception, which is a more subtle and dangerous thing. Is the lady herself writing, or is there, as she avers, a power that controls her, even as the chronicler of the Jews in the Bible averred that he was controlled? In the case of L.S. there is no denying that some messages proved to be not true—especially in the matter of time they were quite unreliable. But on the other hand, the numbers which did come true were far beyond what any guessing or coincidence could account for. Thus, when the *Lusitania* was sunk and the morning papers here announced that so far as known there was no loss of life, the medium at once wrote: "It is terrible, terrible—and will have a great influence on the War." Since it was the first strong impulse which turned America towards the War, the message was true in both respects. Again, she foretold the arrival of an important telegram upon a certain day, and even gave the name of the deliverer of it—a most unlikely person. Altogether, no one could doubt the reality of her inspiration, though the lapses were notable. It was like getting a good message through a very imperfect telephone.

One other incident of the early war days stands out in my memory. A lady in whom I was interested had died in a provincial town. She was a chronic invalid and morphia was found by her bedside. There was an inquest with an open verdict. Eight days later I went to have a sitting with Mr. Vout Peters. After giving me a good deal which was vague and irrelevant, he suddenly said: "There is a lady here. She is leaning upon an older woman. She keeps saying 'Morphia.' Three times she has said it. Her mind was clouded. She did not mean it. Morphia!" Those were almost his exact words. Telepathy was out of the question, for I had entirely other thoughts in my mind at the time and was expecting no such message.

Apart from personal experiences, this movement must gain great additional solidity from the wonderful literature which has sprung up around it during the last few years. If no other spiritual books were in existence than five which I have appeared in the last year or so—I allude to Professor Lodge's *Raymond,* Arthur Hill's *Psychical Investigations,* Professor Crawford's *Reality of Psychical Phenomena,* Professor Barrett's *Threshold of the Unseen,* and Gerald Balfour's *Ear of Dionysius*—those five alone would, in my opinion, be sufficient to establish the facts for any reasonable enquirer.

Before going into this question of a new religious revelation, how it is reached, and what it consists of, I would say a word upon one other subject. There have always been two lines of attack by our opponents. The one is that our facts are not true. This I have dealt with. The other is that we are upon forbidden ground and should come off it and leave it alone. As I started from a position of comparative Materialism, this objection has never had any meaning for me, but to others I would submit one or two considerations. The chief is that God has given us no power at all which is under no circumstances to be used. The fact that we possess it is in itself proof that it is our bounden duty to study and to develop it. It is true that this, like every other power, may be abused if we lose our general sense of proportion and of reason. But I repeat that its mere possession is a strong reason why it is lawful and binding that it be used.

It must also be remembered that this cry of illicit knowledge, backed by more or less appropriate texts, has been used against every advance of human knowledge. It was used against the new astronomy, and Galileo had actually to recant. It was used against Galvani and electricity. It was used against Darwin, who would certainly have been burned had he lived a few centuries before. It was even used against Simpson's use of chloroform in child-birth, on the ground that the Bible declared "in pain shall ye bring them forth." Surely a plea which has been made so often, and so often abandoned, cannot be regarded very seriously.

To those, however, to whom the theological aspect is still a stumbling block, I would recommend the reading of two short books, each of them by clergymen. The one is the Rev. Fielding Ould's *Is Spiritualism of the Devil,* purchasable for twopence; the other is the Rev. Arthur Chambers' *Our Self After Death.* I can also recommend the Rev. Charles Tweedale's writings upon the subject. I may add that when I first began to make public my own views, one of the first letters of sympathy which I received was from the late Archdeacon Wilberforce.

There are some theologians who are not only opposed to such a cult, but who go the length of saying that the phenomena and messages come from friends who personate our dead, or who pretend to be heavenly teachers. It is difficult to think that those who hold this view have ever had any personal experience of the consoling and uplifting effect of such communications upon the recipient. Ruskin has left it on the record that his conviction of a future life came from Spiritualism, though he somewhat ungratefully and illogically added that having got that, he wished to have no more to do with it. There are many, however—quorum pars parva sum [of whom I am a small part]—who without any reserve can declare that they were turned from Materialism to a belief in future life, with all that that implies, by the study of this subject. If this be the devil's work one can only say that the devil seems to be a very bungling workman and to get results very far from what he might be expected to desire.

CHAPTER II

The Revelation

I CAN NOW TURN WITH SOME RELIEF to a more impersonal view of this great subject. Allusion has been made to a body of fresh doctrine. Whence does this come? It comes in the main through automatic writing where the hand of the human medium is controlled, either by an alleged dead human being, as in the case of Miss Julia Ames, or by an alleged higher teacher, as in that of Mr. Stainton Moses. These written communications are supplemented by a vast number of trance utterances, and by the verbal messages of spirits, given through the lips of mediums. Sometimes it has even come by direct voices, as in the numerous cases detailed by Admiral Usborne Moore in his book *The Voices*. Occasionally it has come through the family circle and table-tilting, as, for example, in the two cases I have previously detailed within my own experience. Sometimes, as in a case recorded by Mrs. de Morgan, it has come through the hand of a child.

Now, of course, we are at once confronted with the obvious objection—how do we know that these messages are really from beyond? How do we know that the medium is not consciously writing, or if that be improbable, that he or she is unconsciously writing them by his or her own higher self? This is a perfectly just criticism, and it is one which we must rigorously apply in every case, since if the whole world is to become full of minor prophets, each of them stating their own views of the religious state with no proof save their own assertion, we should, indeed, be back in the dark ages of implicit faith. The answer must be that we require signs which we can test before we accept assertions which we cannot test. In old days they demanded a sign from a prophet, and it was a perfectly reasonable request, and still holds good. If a person comes to me with an account of life in some further world, and has no credentials save his own assertion, I would rather have it in my waste-paper-basket than on my study table. Life is too short to weigh the merits of such productions. But if, as in the case of Stainton Moses, with his *Spirit Teachings,* the doctrines which are said to come from beyond are accompanied with a great number of abnormal gifts—and Stainton Moses was one of the greatest mediums in all ways that England has ever produced—then I look upon the matter in a more serious light. Again, if Miss Julia Ames can tell Mr. Stead things in her own earth life of which he could not have cognisance, and if those things are shown, when tested, to be true, then one is more inclined to think that those things which cannot be tested are true also. Or once again, if Raymond [in *Raymond* by Oliver Lodge] can tell us of a photograph no copy of which had reached England, and which proved to be exactly as he described it, and if he can give us, through the lips of strangers, all sorts of details of his home life, which his own relatives had to verify before they found them to be true, is it unreasonable to suppose that he is fairly accurate in his description of his own experiences and state of life at the very moment at which he is communicating? Or when Mr. Arthur Hill receives messages from folk of whom he never heard, and afterwards verifies that they are true in every detail, is it not a fair inference that they are speaking truths also when they give any light upon their present condition?

The cases are manifold, and I mention only a few of them, but my point is that the whole of this system, from the lowest physical phenomenon of a table-rap up to the most inspired utterance of a prophet, is one complete whole, each link attached to the next one, and that when the humbler end of that chain was placed in the hand of humanity, it was in order that they might, by diligence and reason, feel their way up it until they reached the revelation which waited in the end. Do not sneer at the humble beginnings, the heaving table or the flying tambourine, however much such phenomena may have been abused or simulated, but remember that a falling apple taught us gravity, a boiling kettle brought us the steam engine, and the twitching leg of a frog opened up the train of thought and experiment which gave us electricity. So the lowly manifestations of Hydesville have ripened into results which have engaged the finest group of intellects in this country during the last twenty years, and which are destined, in my opinion, to bring about far the greatest development of human experience which the world has ever seen.

It has been asserted by men for whose opinion I have a deep regard—notably by Sir William Barratt—that psychical research is quite distinct from religion. Certainly it is so, in the sense that a man might be a very good psychical researcher but a very bad man. But the results of psychical research, the deductions which we may draw, and the lessons we may learn, teach us of the continued life of the soul, of the nature of that life, and of how it is influenced by our conduct here. If this is distinct from religion, I must confess that I do not understand the distinction. To me it *is* religion—the very essence of it. But that does not mean that it will necessarily crystallise into a new religion. Personally I trust that it will not do so. Surely we are disunited enough already? Rather would I see it the great unifying force, the one provable thing connected with every religion, Christian or non-Christian, forming the common solid basis upon which each raises, if it must needs raise, that separate system which appeals to the varied types of mind. The Southern races will always demand what is less austere than the North, the West will always be more critical than the East. One cannot shape all to a level conformity. But if the broad premises which are guaranteed by this teaching from beyond are accepted, then the human race has made a great stride towards religious peace and unity. The question which faces us, then, is how will this influence bear upon the older organised religions and philosophies which have influenced the actions of men?

The answer is, that to only one of these religions or philosophies is this New Revelation absolutely fatal. That is to Materialism. I do not say this in any spirit of hostility to Materialists, who, so far as they are an organised body, are, I think, as earnest and moral as any other class. But the fact is manifest that if spirit can live without matter, then the foundation of Materialism is gone, and the whole scheme of thought crashes to the ground.

As to other creeds, it must be admitted that an acceptance of the teaching brought to us from beyond would deeply modify conventional Christianity. But these modifications would be rather in the direction of explanation and development than of contradiction. It would set right grave misunderstandings which have always offended the reason of every thoughtful man, but it would also confirm and make absolutely certain the fact of life after death, the base of all religion. It would confirm the unhappy results of sin, though it would show that those results are never absolutely permanent. It would confirm the existence of higher beings, whom we have called angels, and of an ever-ascending hierarchy above us, in which the Christ Spirit finds its place, culminating in heights of the infinite with which we associate the idea of all-power or of God. It would confirm the idea of heaven and of a temporary penal state which corresponds to purgatory rather than to hell. Thus this New Revelation, on some of the most vital points, is *not* destructive of the beliefs, and it should be hailed by really earnest men of all creeds as a most powerful ally rather than a dangerous devil-begotten enemy.

On the other hand, let us turn to the points in which Christianity must be modified by this New Revelation.

First of all I would say this, which must be obvious to many, however much they deplore it: Christianity must change or must perish. That is the law of life—that things must adapt themselves or perish. Christianity has deferred the change very long, she has deferred it until her churches are half empty, until women are her chief supporters, and until both the learned part of the community on one side, and the poorest class on the other, both in town and country, are largely alienated from her. Let us try and trace the reason for this. It is apparent in all sects, and comes, therefore, from some deep common cause.

People are alienated because they frankly do not believe the facts as presented to them to be true. Their reason and their sense of justice are equally offended. One can see no justice in a vicarious sacrifice, nor in the God who could be placated by such means. Above all, many cannot understand such expressions as the "redemption from sin," "cleansed by the blood of the Lamb," and so forth. So long as there was any question of the fall of man there was at least some sort of explanation of such phrases; but when it became certain that man had never fallen—when with ever fuller knowledge we could trace our ancestral course down through the cave-man and the drift-man, back to that shadowy and far-off time when the man-like ape slowly evolved into the ape-like man—looking back on all this vast succession of life, we knew that it had always been rising from step to step. Never was there any evidence of a fall. But if there were no fall, then what became of the atonement, of the redemption, of original sin, of a large part of Christian mystical philosophy? Even if it were as reasonable in itself as it is actually unreasonable, it would still be quite divorced from the facts.

Again, too much seemed to be made of Christ's death. It is no uncommon thing to die for an idea. Every religion has equally had its martyrs. Men die continually for their convictions. Thousands of our lads are doing it at this instant in France. Therefore the death of Christ, beautiful as it is in the Gospel narrative, has seemed to assume an undue importance, as though it were an isolated phenomenon for a man to die in pursuit of a reform. In my opinion, far too much stress has been laid upon Christ's death, and far too little upon His life. That was where the true grandeur and the true lesson lay. It was a life which even in those limited records shows us no trait which is not beautiful—a life full of easy tolerance for others, of kindly charity, of broad-minded moderation, of gentle courage, always progressive and open to new ideas, and yet never bitter to those ideas which He was really supplanting, though He did occasionally lose His temper with their more bigoted and narrow supporters. Especially one loves His readiness to get at the spirit of religion, sweeping aside the texts and the forms. Never had anyone such a robust common sense, or such a sympathy for weakness. It was this most wonderful and uncommon life, and not his death, which is the true centre of the Christian religion.

Now, let us look at the light which we get from the spirit guides upon this question of Christianity. Opinion is not absolutely uniform yonder, any more than it is here; but reading a number of messages upon this subject, they amount to this: There are many higher spirits with our departed. They vary in degree. Call them "angels," and you are in touch with old religious thought. High above all these is the greatest spirit of whom they have cognisance—not God, since God is so infinite that He is not within their ken—but one who is nearer God and to that extent represents God. This is the Christ Spirit. His special care is the earth. He came down upon it at a time of great earthly depravity—a time when the world was almost as wicked as it is now, in order to give the people the lesson of an ideal life. Then He returned to His own high station, having left an example which is still occasionally followed. That is the story of Christ as spirits have described it. There is nothing here of atonement or redemption. But there is a perfectly feasible and reasonable scheme, which I, for one, could readily believe.

If such a view of Christianity were generally accepted, and if it were enforced by assurance and demonstration from the New Revelation which is coming to us from the other side, then we should have a creed which might unite the churches, which might be reconciled to Science, which might defy all attacks, and which might carry the Christian Faith on for an indefinite period. Reason and Faith would at last be reconciled, a nightmare would be lifted from our minds, and spiritual peace would prevail. I do not see such results coming as a sudden conquest or a violent revolution. Rather will it come as a peaceful penetration, as some crude ideas, such as the Eternal Hell idea, have already gently faded away within our own lifetime. It is, however, when the human soul is ploughed and harrowed by suffering that the seeds of truth may be planted, and so some future spiritual harvest will surely rise from the days in which we live.

When I read the New Testament with the knowledge which I have of Spiritualism, I am left with a deep conviction that the teaching of Christ was in many most important respects lost by the early Church, and has not come down to us. All these allusions to a conquest over death have, as it seems to me, little meaning in the present Christian philosophy, whereas for those who have seen, however dimly, through the veil, and touched, however slightly, the outstretched hands beyond, death has indeed been conquered.

When we read so many references to the phenomena with which we are familiar, the levitations, the tongues of fire, the rushing wind, the spiritual gifts, the working of wonders, we feel that the central fact of all, the continuity of life and the communication with the dead, was most certainly known. Our attention is arrested by such a saying as: "Here He worked no wonders because the people were wanting in faith." Is this not absolutely in accordance with psychic law as we know it? Or when Christ, on being touched by the sick woman, said: "Who has touched me? Much virtue has passed out of me." Could He say more clearly what a healing medium would say now, save that He would use the word "power" instead of "virtue"; or when we read: "Try the spirits whether they be of God," is it not the very advice which would now be given to a novice approaching a séance? It is too large a question for me to do more than indicate, but I believe that this subject, which the more rigid Christian churches now attack so bitterly, is really the central teaching of Christianity itself. To those who would read more upon this line of thought, I strongly recommend Dr. Abraham Wallace's *Jesus of Nazareth,* if this valuable little work is not out of print. He demonstrates in it most convincingly that Christ's miracles were all within the powers of psychic law as we now understand it, and were on the exact lines of such law even in small details. Two examples have already been given. Many are worked out in that pamphlet.

One which convinced me as a truth was the thesis that the story of the materialisation of the two prophets upon the mountain was extraordinarily accurate when judged by psychic law. There is the fact that Peter, James and John (who formed the psychic circle when the dead was restored to life, and were presumably the most helpful of the group) were taken. Then there is the choice of the high pure air of the mountain, the drowsiness of the attendant mediums, the transfiguring, the shining robes, the cloud, the words: "Let us make three tabernacles," with its alternate reading: "Let us make three booths or cabinets" (the ideal way of condensing power and producing materialisations)—all these make a very consistent theory of the nature of the proceedings. For the rest, the list of gifts which St. Paul gives as being necessary for the Christian Disciple, is simply the list of gifts of a very powerful medium, including prophecy, healing, causing miracles (or psychic phenomena), clairvoyance, and other powers (I Corinth, xii, 8, 11). The early Christian Church was saturated with Spiritualism, and they seem to have paid no attention to those Old Testament prohibitions which were meant to keep these powers only for the use and profit of the priesthood.

CHAPTER III

The Coming Life

Now, leaving this large and possibly contentious subject of the modifications which such new revelations must produce in Christianity, let us try to follow what occurs to man after death. The evidence on this point is fairly full and consistent. Messengers from the dead have been received in many lands at various times, mixed up with a good deal about this world, which we could verify. When messages come thus, it is only fair, I think, to suppose that if what we can test is true, then what we cannot test is true also. When in addition we find a very great uniformity in the messages and an agreement as to details which are not at all in accordance with any pre-existing scheme of thought, then I think the presumption of truth is very strong. It is difficult to think that some fifteen or twenty messages from various sources of which I have personal notes, all agree, and yet are all wrong, nor is it easy to suppose that spirits can tell the truth about our world but untruth about their own.

I received lately, in the same week, two accounts of life in the next world, one received through the hand of the near relative of a high dignitary of the Church, while the other came through the wife of a working mechanician in Scotland. Neither could have been aware of the existence of the other, and yet the two accounts are so alike as to be practically the same. [See "Automatic Writing," pages 65–66.]

The message upon these points seems to me to be infinitely reassuring, whether we regard our own fate or that of our friends. The departed all agree that passing is usually both easy and painless, and followed by an enormous reaction of peace and ease. The individual finds himself in a spirit body, which is the exact counterpart of his old one, save that all disease, weakness, or deformity has passed from it. This body is standing or floating beside the old body, and conscious both of it and of the surrounding people. At this moment the dead man is nearer to matter than he will ever be again, and hence it is that at that moment the greater part of those cases occur where, his thoughts having turned to someone in the distance, the spirit body went with the thoughts and was manifest to the person. Out of some 250 cases carefully examined by Mr. Gurney, 134 of such apparitions were actually at this moment of dissolution, when one could imagine that the new spirit body was possibly so far material as to be more visible to a sympathetic human eye than it would later become.

These cases, however, are very rare in comparison with

Automatic Writing

This form of mediumship gives the very highest results, and yet in its very nature is liable to self-deception. Are we using our own hand or is an outside power directing it? It is only by the information received that we can tell, and even then we have to make broad allowance for the action of our own subconscious knowledge. It is worth while perhaps to quote what appears to me to be a thoroughly critic-proof case, so that the inquirer may see how strong the evidence is that these messages are not self-evolved.

This case is quoted in Mr. Arthur Hill's recent book *Man Is a Spirit* (Cassell & Co.) and is contributed by a gentleman who takes the name of Captain James Burton. He is, I understand, the same medium (amateur) through whose communications the position of the buried ruins at Glastonbury have recently been located. "A week after my father's funeral I was writing a business letter, when something seemed to intervene between my hand and the motor centres of my brain, and the hand wrote at an amazing rate a letter, signed with my father's signature and purporting to come from him. I was upset, and my right side and arm became cold and numb. For a year after this letters came frequently, and always at unexpected times. I never knew what they contained until I examined them with a magnifying-glass: they were microscopic. And they contained a vast amount of matter with which it was impossible for me to be acquainted. . . . Unknown to me, my mother, who was staying some sixty miles away, lost her pet dog, which my father had given her. The same night I had a letter from him condoling with her, and stating that the dog was now with him. 'All things which love us and are necessary to our happiness in the world are with us here.' A most sacred secret, known to no one but my father and mother, concerning a matter which occurred years before I was born, was afterwards told me in the script, with the comment: 'Tell your mother this, and she will know that is I, your father, who am writing.' My mother had been unable to accept the possibility up to now, but when I told her this she collapsed and fainted. From that moment the letters became her greatest comfort, for they were lovers during the forty years of their married life, and his death almost broke her heart.

"As for myself, I am as convinced that my father, in his original personality, still exists, as if he were still in his study with the door shut. He is no more dead than he would be were he living in America.

"I have compared the diction and vocabulary of these letters with those employed in my own writing—I am not unknown as a magazine contributor—and I find no points of similarity between the two."

There is much further evidence in this case for which I refer the reader to the book itself.

the total number of deaths. In most cases I imagine that the dead man is too preoccupied with his own amazing experience to have much thought for others. He soon finds, to his surprise, that though he endeavours to communicate with those whom he sees, his ethereal voice and his ethereal touch are equally unable to make any impression upon those human organs which are only attuned to coarser stimuli. It is a fair subject for speculation, whether a fuller knowledge of those light rays which we know to exist on the other side of the spectrum, or of those sounds which we can prove by the vibrations of a diaphragm to exist, although they are too high for mortal ear, may not bring us some further psychical knowledge. Setting that aside, however, let us follow the fortunes of the departing spirit. He is presently aware that there are others in the room besides those who were there in life, and among these others, who seem to him as substantial as the living, there appear familiar faces, and he finds his hand grasped or his lips kissed by those whom he had loved and lost. Then in their company, and with the help and guidance of some more radiant being who has stood by and waited for the newcomer, he drifts to his own surprise through all solid obstacles and out upon his new life.

This is a definite statement, and this is the story told by one after the other with a consistency which impels belief. It is already very different from any old theology. The spirit is not a glorified angel or goblin damned, but it is simply the person himself, containing all his strength and weakness, his wisdom and his folly, exactly as he has retained his personal appearance. We can well believe that the most frivolous and foolish would be awed into decency by so tremendous an experience, but impressions soon become blunted, the old nature may soon reassert itself in new surroundings, and the frivolous still survive, as our séance rooms can testify.

And now, before entering upon his new life, the new spirit has a period of sleep which varies in its length, sometimes hardly existing at all, at others extending for weeks or months. Raymond Lodge [in *Raymond* by Oliver Lodge] said that his lasted for six days. That was the period also in a case of which I had some personal evidence. Mr. Myers, on the other hand, said that he had a very prolonged period of unconsciousness. I could imagine that the length is regulated by the amount of trouble or mental preoccupation of this life, the longer rest giving the better means of wiping this out. Probably the little child would need no such interval at all. This, of course, is pure speculation, but there is a considerable consensus of opinion as to the existence of a period of oblivion after the first impression of the new life and before entering upon its duties.

Having wakened from this sleep, the spirit is weak, as the child is weak after earth birth. Soon, however, strength returns and the new life begins. This leads us to the consideration of heaven and hell. Hell, I may say, drops out altogether, as it has long dropped out of the thoughts of every reasonable man. This odious conception, so blasphemous in its view of the Creator, arose from the exaggerations of Oriental phrases, and may perhaps have been of service in a coarse age where men were frightened by fires, as wild beasts are scared by the travellers. Hell as a permanent place does not exist. But the idea of punishment, of purifying chastisement, in fact of Purgatory, is justified by the reports from the other side. Without such punishment there could be no justice in the Universe, for how impossible it would be to imagine that the fate of a Rasputin is the same as that of a Father Damien. The punishment is very certain and very serious, though in its less severe forms it only consists in the fact that the grosser souls are in lower spheres with a knowledge that their own deeds have placed them there, but also with the hope that expiation and the help of those above them will educate them and bring them level with the others. In this saving process the higher spirits find part of their employment. Miss Julia Ames in her beautiful posthumous book, says in memorable words: "The greatest joy of Heaven is emptying Hell."

Setting aside those probationary spheres, which should perhaps rather be looked upon as a hospital for weakly souls than as a penal community, the reports from the other world are all agreed as to the pleasant conditions of life in the beyond. They agree that like goes to like, that all who love or who have interests in common are united, that life is full of interest and of occupation, and that they would by no means desire to return. All of this is surely tidings of great joy, and I repeat that it is not a vague faith or hope, but that it is supported by all the laws of evidence which agree that where many independent witnesses give a similar account, that account has a claim to be considered a true one. If it were an account of glorified souls purged instantly from all human weakness and of a constant ecstasy of adoration round the throne of the All Powerful, it might well be suspected as being the mere reflection of that popular theology which all the mediums had equally received in their youth. It is, however, very different to any pre-existing system. It is also supported, as I have already pointed out, not merely by the consistency of the accounts, but by the fact that the accounts are the ultimate product of a long series of phenomena, all of which have been attested as true by those who have carefully examined them.

In connection with the general subject of life after death, people may say we have got this knowledge already through faith. But faith, however beautiful in the individual, has always in collective bodies been a very two-edged quality. All would be well if every faith were alike and the intuitions of the human race were constant. We know that it is not so. Faith means to say that you entirely believe a thing which you cannot prove. One man says: "My faith is *this.*" Another says: "My faith is *that.*" Neither can prove it, so they wrangle for ever, either mentally or in the old days physically. If one is stronger than the other, he is inclined to persecute him just to twist him round to the true faith. Because Philip the Second's faith was strong and clear he, quite logically, killed a hundred thousand Lowlanders in the hope that their fellow countrymen would be turned to the all-important truth. Now, if it were recognised that it is by no means virtuous to claim what you could not prove, we should then be driven to observe facts, to reason from them, and perhaps reach common agreement. That is why this psychical movement appears so valuable. Its feet are on something more solid than texts or traditions or intuitions. It is religion from the double point of view of both worlds up to date, instead of the ancient traditions of one world.

We cannot look upon this coming world as a tidy Dutch garden of a place which is so exact that it can easily be described. It is probable that those messengers who come back to us are all, more or less, in one state of development and represent the same wave of life as it recedes from our shores. Communications usually come from those who have not long passed over, and tend to grow fainter, as one would expect. It is instructive in this respect to notice that Christ's reappearances to his disciples or to Paul, are said to have been within a very few years of his death, and that there is no claim among the early Christians to have seen him later.

The cases of spirits who give good proof of authenticity and yet have passed some time are not common. There is, in Mr. Dawson Roger's life, a very good case of a spirit who called himself Manton, and claimed to have been born at Lawrence Lydiard and buried at Stoke Newington in 1677. It was clearly shown afterwards that there was such a man, and that he was Oliver Cromwell's chaplain. So far as my own reading goes, this is the oldest spirit who is on record as returning, and generally they are quite recent. Hence, one gets all one's views from the one generation, as it were, and we cannot take them as final, but only as partial.

How spirits may see things in a different light as they progress in the other world is shown by Miss Julia Ames, who was deeply impressed at first by the necessity of forming a bureau of communication, but admitted, after fifteen years, that not one spirit in a million among the main body upon the other side ever wanted to communicate with us at all since their own loved ones had come over. She had been misled by the fact that when she first passed over everyone she met was newly arrived like herself.

Thus the account we give may be partial, but still such as it is very consistent and of extraordinary interest, since it refers to our own destiny and that of those we love. All agree that life beyond is for a limited period, after which they pass on to yet other phases, but apparently there is more communication between these phases than there is between us and Spiritland. The lower cannot ascend, but the higher can descend at will. The life has a close analogy to that of this world at its best. It is pre-eminently a life of the mind, as this is of the body. Preoccupations of food, money, lust, pain, etc., are of the body and are gone. Music, the Arts, intellectual and spiritual knowledge, and progress have increased. The people are clothed, as one would expect, since there is no reason why modesty should disappear with our new forms. These new forms are the absolute reproduction of the old ones at their best, the young growing up and the old reverting until all come to the normal. People live in communities, as one would expect if like attracts like, and the male spirit still finds his true mate though there is no sexuality in the grosser sense and no childbirth. Since connections still endure, and those in the same state of development keep abreast, one would expect that nations are still roughly divided from each other, though language is no longer a bar, since thought has become a medium of conversation.

How close is the connection between kindred souls over there is shown by the way in which Myers, Gurney and Roden Noel, all friends and co-workers on earth, sent messages together through Mrs. Holland, who knew none of them, each message being characteristic to those who knew the men in life—or the way in which Professor Verrall and Professor Butcher, both famous Greek scholars, collaborated to produce the Greek problem which has been analysed by Mr. Gerald Balfour in *The Ear of Dionysius,* with the result that that excellent authority testified that the effect *could* have been attained by no other entities, save only Verrall and Butcher. It may be remarked in passing that these and other examples show clearly either that the spirits have the use of an excellent reference library or else that they have memories which produce something like omniscience. No human memory could possibly carry all the exact quotations which occur in such communications as *The Ear of Dionysius*.

These, roughly speaking, are the lines of life beyond in its simplest expression, for it is not all simple, and we catch dim glimpses of endless circles below descending into gloom and endless circles above, ascending into glory, all improving, all purposeful, all intensely alive. All are agreed that no religion upon earth has any advantage over another, but that character and refinement are everything. At the same time, all are also in agreement that all religions which inculcate prayer, and an upward glance rather than eyes for ever on the level, is good. In this sense, and in no other—as a help to spiritual life—every form may have a purpose for somebody. If to twirl a brass cylinder forces the Tibetan to admit that there is something higher than his mountains, and more precious than his yaks, then to that extent it is good. We must not be censorious in such matters.

There is one point which may be mentioned here which

is at first startling and yet must commend itself to our reason when we reflect upon it. This is the constant assertion from the other side that the newly passed do not know that they are dead, and that it is a long time, sometimes a very long time, before they can be made to understand it. All of them agree that this state of bewilderment is harmful and retarding to the spirit, and that some knowledge of the actual truth upon this side is the only way to make sure of not being dazed upon the other. Finding conditions entirely different from anything for which either scientific or religious teaching had prepared them, it is no wonder that they look upon their new sensations as some strange dream, and the more rigidly orthodox have been their views, the more impossible do they find it to accept these new surroundings with all that they imply. For this reason, as well as for many others, this New Revelation is a very needful thing for mankind. A smaller point of practical importance is that the aged should realise that it is still worth while to improve their minds, for though they have no time to use their fresh knowledge in this world it will remain as part of their mental outfit in the next. [See "The Next Phase of Life," pages 75–77.]

As to the smaller details of this life beyond, it is better perhaps not to treat them, for the very good reason that they are small details. We will learn them all soon for ourselves, and it is only vain curiosity which leads us to ask for them now. One thing is clear: there are higher intelligences over yonder to whom synthetic chemistry, which not only makes the substance but moulds the form, is a matter of absolute ease. We see them at work in the coarser media, perceptible

The Next Phase of Life

I have spoken in the text of the striking manner in which accounts of life in the next phase, though derived from the most varied and independent sources, are still in essential agreement—an agreement which occasionally descends to small details. A variety is introduced by that fuller vision which can see and describe more than one plane, but the accounts of that happy land to which the ordinary mortal may hope to aspire, are very consistent. Since I wrote the statement I have read three fresh independent descriptions which again confirm the point. One is the account given by "A King's Counsel" in the recent book *I Heard a Voice* (Kegan Paul), which I recommend to inquirers, though it has a strong Roman Catholic bias running through it which shows that our main lines of thought are persistent. A second is the little book *The Light on the Future,* giving the very interesting details of the beyond, gathered by an earnest and reverent circle in Dublin. The other came in a private letter from Mr. Hubert Wales, and is, I think, most instructive. Mr. Wales is a cautious and rather sceptical inquirer who had put away his results with incredulity (he had received them through his own automatic writing). On reading my account of the conditions described in the beyond, he hunted up his own old script which had commended itself so little to him when he first produced it. He says: "After reading your article, I was struck, almost startled, by the circumstance that the statements which had purported to be made to me regarding conditions after death coincided—I think almost to the smallest detail—with those you set out as the result of your collation of material obtained from a great number of sources. I cannot think there was anything in my antecedent reading to account for this coincidence. I had certainly read nothing you had published on the subject. I had purposely avoided *Raymond* and books like it, in order not to vitiate my own results, and the *Proceedings* of the S.P.R. [Society of Psychical Research] which I had read at that time, do not touch, as you know, upon after-death conditions. At any rate I obtained, at various times, statements (as my contemporary notes show) to the effect that, in this persisting state of existence, they have bodies which, though imperceptible by our senses, are as solid to them as ours to us, that these bodies are based on the general characteristics of our present bodies but beautified; that they have no age, no pain, no rich and poor; that they wear clothes and take nourishment; that they do not sleep (though they spoke of passing occasionally into a semi-conscious state which they called 'lying asleep'—a condition, it just occurs to me, which seems to correspond roughly with the 'Hypnoidal' state); that, after a period which is usually shorter than the average life-time here, they pass to some further state of existence; that people of similar thoughts, tastes and feelings, gravitate together; that married couples do not necessarily reunite, but that the love of man and woman continues and is freed of elements which with us often militate against its perfect realisation; that immediately after death people pass into a semi-conscious rest-state lasting various periods, that they are unable to experience bodily

> pain, but are susceptible at times to some mental anxiety; that a painful death is 'absolutely unknown,' that religious beliefs make no difference whatever in the after-state, and that their life altogether is intensely happy, and no one having ever realised it could wish to return here. I got no reference to 'work' by that word, but much to the various interests that were said to occupy them. That is probably only another way of saying the same thing. 'Work' with us has come usually to mean 'work to live,' and that, I was emphatically informed, was not the case with them—that all the requirements of life were somehow mysteriously 'provided.' Neither did I get any reference to a definite 'temporary penal state,' but I gathered that people begin there at the point of intellectual and moral development where they leave off here; and since their state of happiness was based mainly upon sympathy, those who came over in a low moral condition, failed at first for various lengths of time to have the capacity to appreciate and enjoy it."

to our material senses, in the séance room. If they can build up simulacra [vague resemblances] in the séance room, how much may we expect them to do when they are working upon ethereal objects in that ether which is their own medium? It may be said generally that they can make something which is analogous to anything which exists upon earth. How they do it may well be a matter of guess and speculation among the less advanced spirits, as the phenomena of modern science are a matter of guess and speculation to us. If one of us were suddenly called up by the denizen of some sub-human world, and were asked to explain exactly what gravity is, or what magnetism is, how helpless we should be! We may put ourselves in the position, then, of a young engineer soldier like Raymond Lodge, who tries to give some theory of matter in the beyond—a theory which is very likely contradicted by some other spirit who is also guessing at things above him. He may be right, or he may be wrong, but he is doing his best to say what he thinks, as we should do in similar case. He believes that his transcendental chemists can make anything, and that even such unspiritual matter as alcohol or tobacco could come within their powers and could still be craved for by unregenerate spirits. This has tickled the critics to such an extent that one would really think to read the comments that it was the only statement in a book which contains 400 closely-printed pages. Raymond may be right or wrong, but the only thing which the incident proves to me is the unflinching courage and honesty of the man who chronicled it, knowing well the handle that he was giving to his enemies.

There are many who protest that this world which is described to us is too material for their liking. It is not as they would desire it. Well, there are many things in this world which seem different from what we desire, but they exist none the less. But when we come to examine this charge of Materialism and try to construct some sort of system which would satisfy the idealists, it becomes a very difficult task. Are we to be mere wisps of gaseous happiness floating about in the air? That seems to be the idea. But if there is no body like our own, and if there is no character like our own, then say what you will, *we* have become extinct. What is it to a mother if some impersonal glorified entity is shown to her? She will say, "that is not the son I lost—I want his yellow hair, his quick smile, his little moods that I know so well." That is what she wants; that, I believe, is what she will have; but she will not have them by any system which cuts us away from all that reminds us of matter and takes us to a vague region of floating emotions.

There is an opposite school of critics which rather finds the difficulty in picturing a life which has keen perceptions, robust emotions, and a solid surrounding all constructed in so diaphanous a material. Let us remember that everything depends upon its comparison with the things around it.

If we could conceive a world a thousand times denser, heavier and duller than this world, we can clearly see that to its inmates it would seem much the same as this, since their strength and texture would be in proportion. If, however, these inmates came in contact with us, they would look upon us as extraordinarily airy beings living in a strange, light, spiritual atmosphere. They would not remember that we also, since our beings and our surroundings are in harmony and in proportion to each other, feel and act exactly as they do.

We have now to consider the case of yet another stratum of life, which is as much above us as the leaden community would be below us. To us also it seems as if these people, these spirits, as we call them, live the lives of vapour and shadows. We do not recollect that there also everything is in proportion and in harmony so that the spirit scene or the spirit dwelling, which might seem a mere dream thing to us, is as actual to the spirit as are our own scenes or our own dwellings, and that the spirit body is as real and tangible to another spirit as ours to our friends.

CHAPTER IV

Problems and Limitations

LEAVING FOR A MOMENT THE larger argument as to the lines of this revelation and the broad proofs of its validity, there are some smaller points which have forced themselves upon my attention during the consideration of the subject. This home of our dead seems to be very near to us—so near that we continually, as they tell us, visit them in our sleep. Much of that quiet resignation which we have all observed in people who have lost those whom they loved—people who would in our previous opinion have been driven mad by such loss—is due to the fact that they have seen their dead, and that although the switch-off is complete and they can recall nothing whatever of the spirit experience in sleep, the soothing result of it is still carried on by the subconscious self. The switch-off is, as I say, complete, but sometimes for some reason it is hung up for a fraction of a second, and it is at such moments that the dreamer comes back from his dream "trailing clouds of glory." From this also come all those prophetic dreams many of which are well attested. I have had a recent personal experience of one which has not yet perhaps entirely justified itself but is even now remarkable.

Upon April 4th of last year, 1917, I awoke with a feeling that some communication had been made to me of which I had only carried back one word which was ringing in my head. That word was "Piave." To the best of my belief I had never heard the word before. As it sounded like the name of a place I went into my study the moment I had dressed and I looked up the index of my Atlas. There was "Piave" sure enough, and I noted that it was a river in Italy some forty miles behind the front line, which at that time was victoriously advancing. I could imagine few more unlikely things than that the War should roll back to the Piave, and I could not think how any military event of consequence could arise there, but none the less I was so impressed that I drew up a statement that some such event would occur there, and I had it signed by my secretary and witnessed by my wife with the date, April 4th, attached. It is a matter of history how six months later the whole Italian line fell back, how it abandoned successive positions upon rivers, and how it stuck upon this stream which was said by military critics to be strategically almost untenable. If nothing more should occur (I write upon February 20th, 1918), the reference to the name has been fully justified, presuming that some friend in the beyond was forecasting the coming events of the War.

I have still a hope, however, that more was meant, and that some crowning victory of the Allies at this spot may justify still further the strange way in which the name was conveyed to my mind.

People may well cry out against this theory of sleep on the grounds that all the grotesque, monstrous and objectionable dreams which plague us cannot possibly come from a high source. On this point I have a very definite theory, which may perhaps be worthy of discussion. I consider that there are two forms of dreams, and only two, the experiences of the released spirit, and the confused action of the lower faculties which remain in the body when the spirit is absent. The former is rare and beautiful, for the memory of it fails us. The latter are common and varied, but usually fantastic or ignoble. By noting what is absent in the lower dreams one can tell what the missing qualities are, and so judge what part of us goes to make up the spirit. Thus in these dreams humour is wanting, since we see things which strike us afterwards as ludicrous, and are not amused. The sense of proportion and of judgment and of aspiration is all gone. In short, the higher is palpably gone, and the lower, the sense of fear, of sensual impression, of self-preservation, is functioning all the more vividly because it is relieved from the higher control.

The limitations of the powers of spirits is a subject which is brought home to one in these studies. People say, "If they exist why don't they do this or that?" The answer usually is that they can't. They appear to have very fixed limitations like our own. This seemed to be very clearly brought out in the cross-correspondence experiments where several writing mediums were operating at a distance quite independently of each other, and the object was to get agreement which was beyond the reach of coincidence. The spirits seem to know exactly what they impress upon the minds of the living, but they do not know how far they carry their instruction out. Their touch with us is intermittent. Thus, in the cross-correspondence experiments we continually have them asking, "Did you get that?" or "Was it all right?" Sometimes they have partial cognisance of what is done, as where Myers says: "I saw the circle, but was not sure about the triangle." It is everywhere apparent that their spirits, even the spirits of those who, like Myers and Hodgson, were in specially close touch with psychic subjects, and knew all that could be done, were in difficulties when they desired to get cognisance of a material thing, such as a written document. Only, I should imagine, by partly materialising themselves could they do so, and they may not have had the power of self-materialisation. This consideration throws some light upon the famous case, so often used by our opponents, where Myers failed to give some word or phrase which had been left behind in a sealed box. Apparently he could not see this document from his present position, and if his memory failed him he would be very likely to go wrong about it.

Many mistakes may, I think, be explained in this fashion. It has been asserted from the other side, and the assertion seems to me reasonable, that when they speak of their own conditions they are speaking of what they know and can readily and surely discuss; but that when we insist (as we must sometimes insist) upon earthly tests, it drags them back to another plane of things, and puts them in a position which is far more difficult, and liable to error.

Another point which is capable of being used against us is this: The spirits have the greatest difficulty in getting names through to us, and it is this which makes many of their communications so vague and unsatisfactory. They will talk all round a thing, and yet never get the name which would clinch the matter. There is an example of the point in a recent communication in *Light,* which describes how a young officer, recently dead, endeavoured to get a message through the direct voice method of Mrs. Susannah Harris to his father. He could not get his name through. He was able, however, to make it clear that his father was a member of the Kildare Street Club in Dublin. Inquiry found the father, and it was then learned that the father had already received an independent message in Dublin to say that an inquiry was coming through from London. I do not know if the earth name is a merely ephemeral thing, quite disconnected from the personality, and perhaps the very first thing to be thrown aside. That is, of course, possible. Or it may be that some law regulates our intercourse from the other side by which it shall not be too direct, and shall leave something to our own intelligence.

This idea, that there is some law which makes an indirect speech more easy than a direct one, is greatly borne out by the cross-correspondences, where circumlocution continually takes the place of assertion. Thus, in the St. Paul correspondence, which is treated in the July pamphlet of the S.P.R. [Society of Psychical Research], the idea of St. Paul was to be conveyed from one automatic writer to two others, both of whom were at a distance, one of them in India. Dr. Hodgson was the spirit who professed to preside over this experiment. You would think that the simple words "St. Paul" occurring in the other scripts would be all-sufficient. But no; he proceeds to make all sorts of indirect allusions, to talk all round St. Paul in each of the scripts, and to make five quotations from St. Paul's writings. This is beyond coincidence, and quite convincing, but none the less it illustrates the curious way in which they go round instead of going straight. If one could imagine some wise angel on the other side saying, "Now, don't make it too easy for these people. Make them use their own brains a little. They will become mere automatons if we do everything for them"—if we could imagine that, it would just cover the case. Whatever the explanation, it is a noteworthy fact.

There is another point about spirit communications which is worth noting. This is their uncertainty wherever any time element comes in. Their estimate of time is almost invariably wrong. Earth time is probably a different idea to spirit time, and hence the confusion. We had the advantage, as I have stated, of the presence of a lady in our household who developed writing mediumship. She was in close touch with three brothers, all of whom had been killed in the War. This lady, conveying messages from her brothers, was hardly ever entirely wrong upon facts, and hardly ever right about time. There was one notable exception, however, which in itself is suggestive. Although her prophecies as to public events were weeks or even months out, she in one case foretold the arrival of a telegram from Africa to the day. Now the telegram had already been sent, but was delayed, so that the inference seems to be that she could foretell a course of events which had actually been set in motion, and calculate how long they would take to reach their end. On the other hand, I am bound to admit that she confidently prophesied the escape of her fourth brother, who was a prisoner in Germany, and that this was duly fulfilled. On the whole I preserve an open mind upon the powers and limitations of prophecy.

But apart from all these limitations we have, unhappily, to deal with absolute cold-blooded lying on the part of wicked or mischievous intelligences. Everyone who has investigated the matter has, I suppose, met with examples of wilful deception, which occasionally are mixed up with good and true communications. It was of such messages, no doubt, that the Apostle wrote when he said: "Beloved, believe not every spirit, but try the spirits whether they are of God." These words can only mean that the early Christians not only practised Spiritualism as we understand it, but also that they were faced by the same difficulties. There is nothing more puzzling than the fact that one may get a long connected description with every detail given, and that it may prove to be entirely a concoction. However, we must bear in mind that if one case comes absolutely correct, it atones for many failures, just as if you had one telegram correct you would know that there was a line and a communicator, however much they broke down afterwards. But it must be admitted that it is very discomposing and makes one sceptical of messages until they are tested. Of a kin with these false influences are all the Miltons who cannot scan, and Shelleys who cannot rhyme, and Shakespeares who cannot think, and all the other absurd impersonations which make our cause ridiculous. They are, I think, deliberate frauds, either from this side or from the other, but to say that they invalidate the whole subject is as senseless as to invalidate our own world because we encounter some unpleasant people.

One thing I can truly say, and that is, that in spite of false messages, I have never in all these years known a blasphemous, an unkind, or an obscene message. Such incidents must be of very exceptional nature. I think also that, so far as allegations concerning insanity, obsession, and so forth go, they are entirely imaginary. Asylum statistics do not bear out such assertions, and mediums live to as good an average age as anyone else. I think, however, that the cult of the séance may be very much overdone. When once you have convinced yourself of the truth of the phenomena the physical séance has done its work, and the man or woman who spends his or her life in running from séance to séance is in danger of becoming a mere sensation hunter. Here, as in other cults, the form is in danger of eclipsing the real thing, and in pursuit of physical proofs one may forget that the real object of all these things is, as I have tried to point out, to give us assurance in the future and spiritual strength in the present, to attain a due perception of the passing nature of matter and the all-importance of that which is immaterial.

The conclusion, then, of my long search after truth, is that in spite of occasional fraud, which Spiritualists deplore, and in spite of wild imaginings, which they discourage, there remains a great solid core in this movement which is infinitely nearer to positive proof than any other religious development with which I am acquainted. As I have shown, it would appear to be a re-discovery rather than an absolutely new thing, but the result in this material age is the same.

The days are surely passing when the mature and considered opinions of such men as Crookes, Wallace, Flammarion, Chas. Richet, Lodge, Barratt, Lombroso, Generals Drayson and Turner, Sergeant Ballantyne, W.T. Stead, Judge Edmunds, Admiral Usborne Moore, the late Archdeacon Wilberforce, and such a cloud of other witnesses, can be dismissed with the empty "All rot" or "Nauseating drivel" formulae. As Mr. Arthur Hill has well said, we have reached a point where further proof is superfluous, and where the weight of disproof lies upon those who deny. The very people who clamour for proofs have as a rule never taken the trouble to examine the copious proofs which already exist. Each seems to think that the whole subject should begin *de novo* [anew] because he has asked for information.

The method of our opponents is to fasten upon the latest man who has stated the case—at the present instant it happens to be Sir Oliver Lodge—and then to deal with him as if he had come forward with some new opinions which rested entirely upon his own assertion, with no reference to the corroboration of so many independent workers before him. This is not an honest method of criticism, for in every case the agreement of witnesses is the very root of conviction. But as a matter of fact, there are many single witnesses upon whom this case could rest. If, for example, our only knowledge of unknown forces depended upon the researches of Dr. Crawford of Belfast, who places his amateur medium in a weighing chair with her feet from the ground, and has been able to register a difference of weight of many pounds, corresponding with the physical phenomena produced, a result which he has tested and recorded in a true scientific spirit of caution, I do not see how it could be shaken. The phenomena are and have long been firmly established for every open mind. One feels that the stage of investigation is passed, and that of religious construction is overdue.

For are we to satisfy ourselves by observing the phenomena with no attention to what the phenomena mean, as group of savages might stare at a wireless installation with no appreciation of the messages coming through it, or are we resolutely to set ourselves to define these subtle and elusive utterances from beyond, and to construct from them a religious scheme, which will be founded upon human reason on this side and upon spirit inspiration upon the other? These phenomena have passed through the stage of being a parlour game; they are now emerging from that of a debatable scientific novelty; and they are, or should be, taking shape as the foundations of a definite system of religious thought, in some ways confirmatory of ancient systems, in some ways entirely new. The evidence upon which this system rests is so enormous that it would take a very considerable library to contain it, and the witnesses are not shadowy people living in the dim past and inaccessible to our cross-examination, but are our own contemporaries, men of character and intellect whom all must respect.

The situation may, as it seems to me, be summed up in a simple alternative. The one supposition is that there has been an outbreak of lunacy extending over two generations of mankind, and two great continents—a lunacy which assails men or women who are otherwise eminently sane. The alternative supposition is that in recent years there has come to us from divine sources a New Revelation which constitutes by far the greatest religious event since the death of Christ (for the Reformation was a re-arrangement of the old, not a revelation of the new), a revelation which alters the whole aspect of death and the fate of man. Between these two suppositions there is no solid position. Theories of fraud or of delusion will not meet the evidence. It is absolute lunacy or it is a revolution in religious thought, a revolution which gives us as by-products an utter fearlessness of death, and an immense consolation when those who are dear to us pass behind the veil.

I should like to add a few practical words to those who know the truth of what I say. We have here an enormous new development, the greatest in the history of mankind. How are we to use it? We are bound in honour, I think, to state our own belief, especially to those who are in trouble. Having stated it, we should not force it, but leave the rest to higher wisdom than our own. We wish to subvert no religion. We wish only to bring back the material-minded—to take them out of their cramped valley and put them on the ridge, whence they can breathe purer air and see other valleys and other ridges beyond. Religions are mostly petrified and decayed, overgrown with forms and choked with mysteries. We can prove that there is no need for this. All that is essential is both very simple and very sure.

The clear call for our help comes from those who have had a loss and who yearn to re-establish connection. This also can be overdone. If your boy were in Australia, you would not expect him to continually stop his work and write long letters at all seasons. Having got in touch, be moderate in your demands. Do not be satisfied with any evidence short of the best, but having got that, you can, it seems to me, wait for that short period when we shall all be re-united. I am in touch at present with thirteen mothers who are in correspondence with their dead sons. In each case, the husband, where he is alive, is agreed as to the evidence. In only one case so far as I know was the parent acquainted with psychic matters before the War.

Several of these cases have peculiarities of their own. In two of them the figures of the dead lads have appeared beside the mothers in a photograph. In one case the first message to the mother came through a stranger to whom the correct address of the mother was given. The communication afterwards became direct. In another case the method of sending messages was to give references to particular pages and lines of books in distant libraries, the whole conveying a message. The procedure was to weed out all fear of telepathy. Verily there is no possible way by which a truth can be proved by which this truth has not been proved.

How are you to act? There is the difficulty. There are true men and there are frauds. You have to work warily. So far as professional mediums go, you will not find it difficult to get recommendations. Even with the best you may draw entirely blank. The conditions are very elusive. And yet some get the result at once. We cannot lay down laws, because the law works from the other side as well as this. Nearly every woman is an undeveloped medium. Let her try her own powers of automatic writing. There again, what is done must be done with every precaution against self-deception, and in a reverent and prayerful mood. But if you are earnest, you will win through somehow, for someone else is probably trying on the other side.

Some people discountenance [disapprove of] communication upon the grounds that it is hindering the advance of the departed. There is not a little of evidence for this. The assertions of the spirits are entirely to the contrary and they declare that they are helped and strengthened by the touch with those whom they love. I know few more moving passages in their simple boyish eloquence than those in which Raymond describes the feelings of the dead boys who want to get messages back to their people and find that ignorance and prejudice are a perpetual bar. "It is hard to think your sons are dead, but such a lot of people do think so. It is revolting to hear the boys tell you how no one speaks of them ever. It hurts me through and through."

Above all read the literature of this subject. It has been far too much neglected, not only by the material world but by believers. Soak yourself with this grand truth. Make yourself familiar with the overpowering evidence. Get away from the phenomenal side and learn the lofty teaching from such beautiful books as *After Death* or from Stainton Moses'

Spirit Teachings. There is a whole library of such literature, of unequal value but of a high average. Broaden and spiritualise your thoughts. Show the results in your lives. Unselfishness, that is the keynote to progress. Realise not as a belief or a faith, but as a fact which is as tangible as the streets of London, that we are moving on soon to another life, that all will be very happy there, and that the only possible way in which that happiness can be marred or deferred is by folly and selfishness in these few fleeting years.

It must be repeated that while the New Revelation may seem destructive to those who hold Christian dogmas with extreme rigidity, it has quite the opposite effect upon the mind which, like so many modern minds, had come to look upon the whole Christian scheme as a huge delusion. It is shown clearly that the old revelation has so many resemblances, defaced by time and mangled by man's mishandling and materialism, but still denoting the same general scheme, that undoubtedly both have come from the same source. The accepted ideas of life after death, of higher and lower spirits, of comparative happiness depending upon our own conduct, of chastening by pain, of guardian spirits, of high teachers, of an infinite central power, of circles above circles approaching nearer to His presence—all of these conceptions appear once more and are confirmed by many witnesses. It is only the claims of infallibility and of monopoly, the bigotry and pedantry of theologians, and the man-made rituals which take the life out of the God-given thoughts—it is only this which has defaced the truth.

I cannot end this little book better than by using words

more eloquent than any which I could write, a splendid sample of English style as well as of English thought. They are from the pen of that considerable thinker and poet, Mr. Gerald Massey, and were written many years ago.

> *"Spiritualism has been for me, in common with many others, such a lifting of the mental horizon and letting-in of the heavens—such a formation of faith into facts, that I can only compare life without it to sailing on board ship with hatches battened down and being kept a prisoner, living by the light of a candle, and then suddenly, on some splendid starry night, allowed to go on deck for the first time to see the stupendous mechanism of the heavens all aglow with the glory of God."*

Afterword

Making and keeping a friend is one of life's mysteries, a complicated process that often intertwines very different personalities. Shortly after Sir Arthur Conan Doyle embraced Spiritualism and wrote *The New Revelation,* he entered into a transatlantic correspondence with magician Harry Houdini (1874–1926). A friendship gradually blossomed between these two men, who were world-renowned. They were drawn together by a common concern with testing the foundations of Spiritualism. As a believer, Doyle held no doubts of the human ability to communicate with departed souls, while Houdini, although professing a willingness to be convinced, found it difficult to accept the validity of that fact. Even as they wrote cordial letters to each other, many of which are excerpted in the following account, both men knew that their budding friendship might disintegrate over fundamental principles.

More personal ties between Doyle and Houdini began during the magician's successful tour of British cities in 1920. In March, the two exchanged copies of their latest books, and offered rival theories as to the abilities of the Davenport Brothers—late nineteenth-century American escape artists famed for their "rope-tie" trick and spiritual manifestations. After appearing at the London Palladium, Houdini performed at Brighton, where Sir Arthur and his family were enthralled by his escapes and illusions. The celebrities finally met, and soon afterwards Houdini asked Doyle to facilitate his meetings with British mediums: "I believe you are one of the most serious men I know on the positive side" of spiritual beliefs. Since Houdini's interest in the spirit world was well known: "I am still a skeptic but a seeker after the Truth," Doyle willingly provided his new American friend with cards of introduction to séances across the British Isles.

Houdini knew that Sir Arthur and his Lady "believe implicitly in spiritualism," and hoped to discover for himself the possibility of communication with departed loved ones. In the succeeding months, Houdini attended over 100 such performances, respectfully never leaving his chair and refusing to act in an intrusive manner. He traced every effect to standard magician trickery. But Doyle refused to accept Houdini's judgment as final, even though he conceded as proven the deceptions of some mediums. Houdini performed a public service when he exposed such fakery, but Sir Arthur believed his friend's emphasis on physical proofs alone was flawed, since it ignored the more valuable mental aspects of Spiritualism.

Despite their different approaches, both men truly enjoyed each other's company. Doyle was so taken by Houdini's performances that he attributed his new friend's escape to occult powers. His letters progressed from wonder: "I can't conceive how you do it. You must be a very brave man as well as extraordinarily dexterous," to a belief in Houdini's psychic powers: "Why go around the world seeking a demonstration of the occult when you are giving one all the time?" Doyle was unable to accept that skill, practice, and physical endurance were Houdini's stock in trade. He believed that Houdini's feats were so far beyond the capability of humans that he must be a medium, and refused to admit his talent. Doyle even came to believe that Houdini had the ability to dematerialize: "My reason tells me you have this wonderful power, for there is no alternative." When Houdini returned home in July, he invited the Doyles to stay in his New York City home during any future tours of North America.

During the 1920s, Doyle became Spiritualism's most prominent advocate, visiting three continents to popularize his beliefs. After arriving in New York in April of 1922, Doyle delivered seven sold-out lectures in Carnegie Hall, but the crowd seemed more interested in seeing the creator of Sherlock Holmes than hearing the message of Spiritualism. *The New York Times* treated Doyle's presentation quite brutally, and Mayor John Hylan mocked the proceedings. Nevertheless Doyle seemed pleased with his public reception, and looked forward to renewing personal ties with Houdini.

Due to the "semi-public" nature of the tour, Doyle declined Houdini's invitation to stay at his home, but asked if he and his wife could see the magician's "psychic library." On

May 10, Doyle attended a pleasant luncheon at the home of his friend, but was disappointed to discover the magician's library contained primarily books of magic. Doyle wrote, " . . . your collection is very short of positive books (on Spiritualism)—you have very few of the really classic books of the pioneers." Houdini played the gracious host. He understood the faith of the Doyles, but expressed his wonder that they "related a number of incidents which they accepted without proof." Even simple magic tricks Houdini performed during a cab ride were attributed to his "wonderful powers, whether inborn or acquired," rather than his dexterity. Hoping to expand Doyle's perceptions, he invited Sir Arthur to attend the annual banquet of the Society of American Magicians in early June, an event the author attended only after being assured that the group did not intend to disparage his beliefs. The event proved a triumph for Doyle, who stunned his audience with realistic films of dinosaurs that were prepared by Hollywood animators. He proudly claimed to have mystified "those who have so often and so successfully mystified others."

In June 1922, the Doyles and the Houdinis spent a seaside weekend together in Atlantic City during which Lady Jean Doyle held a private séance for Houdini. Sir Arthur's wife believed herself to be a medium who could establish communication with Houdini's dead mother through "automatic writing." While the Doyles viewed the séance as a resounding success, Houdini found it highly disappointing. Their very different perceptions became chapters in Houdini's *A Magician Among the Spirits* (1924) and Doyle's *Our American Adventure* (1923). After June 17, 1922, the profound differences between the two men could no longer be papered over in polite correspondence.

Sir Arthur and his family returned to England a few days later, carrying a farewell note from the Houdinis. Doyle considered his trip successful, for he had brought comfort to parents who had lost sons in the war, and he had earned a large fee, part of which he would contribute to spiritualist groups. He was dismayed only when Houdini, on October 30, published an article on Spiritualism in the New York *Sun,* criticizing a New York spiritualist association. It was the magician's assertion that he had no knowledge of "anything that could convince me that there is a possibility of communication with the loved ones who have gone" that outraged Doyle, who interpreted the statement as an implied attack on his wife. "When you say that you have had no evidence of survival, you say what I cannot reconcile with what I saw with my own eyes. I know . . . the purity of my wife's mediumship, and I saw what you got and what the effect was on you at the time." Houdini immediately responded. "I hold both Lady Doyle and yourself in the highest esteem. I know you treat this as a religion but personally I cannot do so." Nevertheless, disagreement over the value of the séance doomed the friendship.

By the time Doyle's lecture tour resumed in April 1923, Houdini had begun to publicly denounce Spiritualism as fraudulent and expose its practices. The two men met in Denver, but the session failed after Houdini told Doyle that he was incapable of detecting any magician's trickery. They sparred in newspaper letters that were published in Denver, Cleveland, and San Francisco. Doyle was implacable: "So long as you attack what I know from experience to be true, I have no alternative but to attack you in return. How long a private friendship can survive such an ordeal I do not know."

Restoration of their former intimacy was impossible, and letters were few in the next two years. Houdini's willingness to serve on the *Scientific American* investigative panel for mediums was the final straw that ruptured the relationship. An outraged Doyle issued a denunciation of the magician (*Boston Herald,* January 26, 1925), which did his reputation little good, and led Houdini to declare him "a bit senile (and) . . . easily bamboozled." The magician judged Doyle to be "good-natured, very bright, but a monomaniac on the subject of Spiritualism."

An author who knew "spirit return to be a fact," and a conjurer who exposed hoaxes would seem to have little in common. Yet their letters show real deference to each other and a willingness to trade information. Houdini's success at exposing medium fakery never affected Doyle's faith in Spiritualism. Their personal rift developed only after a séance whose results were disputed. After Houdini's unexpected death on October 31, 1926, Sir Arthur wrote a moving tribute on the "riddle" of the magician, "a fine and honest man" filled with courage; he also continued to correspond with the magician's widow.

In an introspective letter before his own death, Doyle speculated on the "chance that I may talk it all over with Houdini himself before very long. I view the prospect with perfect equanimity. That is one thing that psychic knowledge does. It removes all fear of the future."

Index

T

V

W

Other Titles of Interest

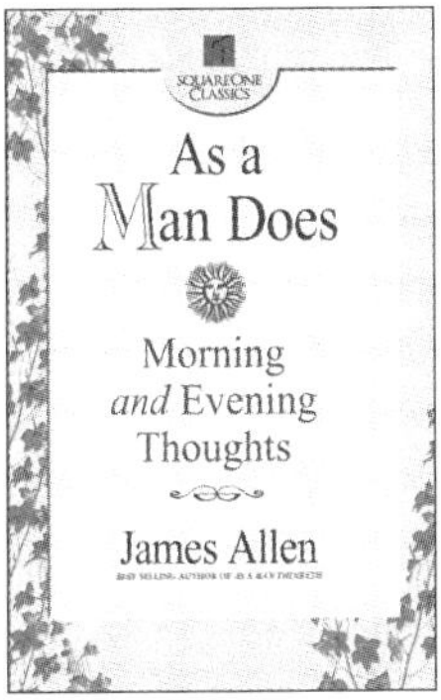

As a Man Does

Morning and Evening Thoughts

James Allen

James Allen is considered to be one of the first great modern writers of motivational and inspirational books. Today, his work *As a Man Thinketh* continues to influence millions around the world. In the same way, his work *As a Man Does: Morning and Evening Thoughts* offers sixty-two beautiful and insightful meditations. Readers will find that each meditation contains both the force of truth and the blessing of comfort.

As a Man Does: Morning and Evening Thoughts was James Allen's last work. It provides the reader with spiritual jewels of wisdom every bit as powerful as those found in *As a Man Thinketh.* The meditations offered in *As a Man Does* reflect the deepest experiences of the heart. As a book, its mission is simple: To lift the soul of its reader—"in the hours of work and leisure, in the days of joy and sorrow, in the sunshine and in the cloud."

As part of Square One's Classics series, we are proud to make available this beautifully packaged title to the millions of readers who have read James Allen's first bestseller, *As a Man Thinketh.* We also believe that the release of *As a Man Does* will find a whole new generation of readers ready to be moved and inspired.

\$8.95 • 144 pgs • $5\frac{1}{2}$ x $8\frac{1}{2}$ inch • Paperback • ISBN 0-7570-0018-5

For a copy of the Square One catalog,
Call us at 516-535-2010
Or visit our website at SQUAREONEPUBLISHERS.COM

Other Titles of Interest

How to Pray

Tapping Into the Power of Divine Communication

Helene Ciaravino

The power of prayer is real. It can heal illness, win battles, and move personal mountains. Cultures and religions throughout the world use their own individual systems of divine communication for comfort, serenity, guidance, and more. Unfortunately, too few of us understand or know how to tap into the power of prayer. *How to Pray* was written for everyone who wants to learn more about this universal practice.

How to Pray begins by widening your perspective on prayer through several intriguing definitions. It then discusses the many scientific studies that have validated the power of prayer, and—to shine a light on any roadblocks that may be hindering you—it discusses common reasons why some people *don't* pray. Part Two examines the history and prayer techniques of four great traditions: Judaism, Christianity, Islam, and Buddhism. In these chapters, you'll learn about the beliefs, practices, and individual prayers that have been revered for centuries. Part Three focuses on the development of your own personal prayer life, first by explaining some easy ways in which you can make your practice of prayer more effective and fulfilling, and then by exploring the challenges of prayer—from seemingly unanswered prayers and spiritual dry spells, to the joyful task of making your whole day a prayer. Finally, a useful resource directory suggests books and websites that provide further information.

If you want to learn more about the use of prayer all over the world; if you are interested in finding wholeness and healing; or if you simply want to enhance the harmony in your life, *How to Pray* will give you the guidance, the knowledge, and the inspiration that you seek.

$13.95 • 264 pgs • 6 x 9 inch • Paperback • ISBN 0-7570-0012-6